MEET MY THREE FRIENDS

Purpose, Passion and Power

DR. TAMARA MANGUM

MEET MY THREE FRIENDS

Purpose, Passion and Power

The Woman's Guide

to Following Passion,

Surrendering to Purpose

& Harnessing Power

DTM Enterprises Management Group, LLC.

This publication is designed to provide competent and reliable information regarding the subject matter covered. This is a work of fiction. Names, characters, places, and incidents either are the products of the author's imagination or are used fictitiously. Any resemblance to actual persons, living or dead, businesses, companies, events, or locales is entirely coincidental.

DTM Enterprises Management Group, LLC.
2004 Morris Ave. Suite 1 Union, NJ 07083

Cover design by Fivver
Cover photography by Daniella Mone Photography
First printing edition 2018.

Ordering Information:
Quantity sales. Special discounts are available on quantity purchases by corporations, associations, and others. For details, contact the publisher at the address above.

ISBN: 978-1-7322222-0-5 (Paperback) 978-1-7322222-1-2 (ebook)

Dr. Tamara Mangum
www.drtamaramangum.com
twitter.com/drtamaramangum
Printed in the United States of America

This book is dedicated to Nyla Amorae, my 11 year old daughter. Find your three best friends sweetheart and hold onto them. Mommy loves you.....

CONTENTS

INTRODUCTION

"There is no greater agony than bearing an untold story inside of you."

—Maya Angelou

I was twenty-three years old and at the top of my game. Recently married and with my Master's degree well behind me, I was living a beautiful life. I had the perfect job, and my career as an account manager with a local telecommunications company had taken off. With a five-figure income, a reasonable salary for someone my age, I was proud of my brief accomplishments and was ready for the next shift in my life. So, the next best logical thing to do was to enroll in a doctoral program.

Eager for growth, I took a job in NYC and shortly after that, 911 took our Nation by storm. I was left without a job, and the uncertainty of my next move was all too disheartening. But the bounce back was surreal. I landed another position in NYC and was happy for the opportunity to once again do what I thought I loved - making money.

By the age of twenty-five, I had launched my first successful business but still worked my full-time job to make it through the rough patches. Balancing the two became very tricky, but I was determined to make it work. Fast forward four years later, tragedy struck our family like a tsunami. My mother was diagnosed with breast cancer, I with Leukemia and I lost one of my favorite younger uncles and a cousin. Oh and I failed to mention, my grandmother and grandfather both died in the same month. The funny thing is, my grandmother always said she'd outlive my grandfather. And that she did, by two weeks.

The blessing in all that sickness and death was that my little family was growing. My husband and I welcomed our first and only child into this world. Now, not only was I responsible for my success, I was responsible for my this little gift that God had given to me.

After the birth of my daughter, I graduated with a Ph.D. and my business had taken a life of its own. With over $2Million in annual revenues, I was overjoyed, and life couldn't have gotten much better. Mom and I were doing well, healing from both our physical and emotional scars. But, my life somehow became turned upside down. I couldn't find my happy place. I could speculate on many reasons for such a drastic change. But, I'm not sure when it happened, how it happened and why it happened. All I know is that I was no longer this bubbly, high spirited soul I once knew.

I remember like it was yesterday. I was at the lowest of my low, and with every passing day, it became harder and harder to rise. I had lost all hope, and my faith had dwindled smaller than a mustard seed. I was living to just function and functioning just to live. I was brazen with fear and emotional pain, stricken by the circumstances and situations I found myself and the people I was connected to and surrounded by. While I still managed to handle my daily business, I felt lost and empty, directionless and misguided. I lacked the luster in the step I once had, and my confidence was at an all-time low. Despite having everything I could have ever wanted, something was still missing.

While I knew I was a work in progress, could I have been broken? But, from what? What was causing these unusual and uncomfortable emotions I was experiencing? Was it something that I was doing to myself or was it something someone was doing to me? These are the questions I'd pose to myself.

So, I began reevaluating everything and everyone in my life that was causing me an ounce of discomfort. I started reading and studying all the self-help, spiritual and women devotional books that I could find. I skimmed through those pages secretly hoping to find the answers that would preclude my assured demise. As I turned each page, I thought to myself this must be it, the solution to my problems would be on the very next line. Many of those books were enriching and gave me morsels of hope. And, other's gave me a boost of confidence and courage to at least try to get up yet another day. But for the times they did not work, I resorted to my past time; I'd get on my knees to pray. However, while in prayer, I found myself questioning God's plan for me. In fact, I thought that He was rejecting me.

My o my, was I doomed. Simply put, I could not see my way through. I was lost, dying a slow death, bleeding from the inside out and didn't even know it. I was afraid to admit that I was sinking. Afraid to admit that I needed help. And, too scared to show the world that in that moment of my life, I was vulnerable and weak.

After wrestling with these demons for what seemed like an eternity, my answer from God would come strong and swift. On a ride home from work, with tears streaming down my face,

I could hear Him clearly say, "I'm not rejecting you, I'm redirecting you. Now, let go and let me drive".

My delivery from these inhibitions came when I began to really let go - let go of the people who meant me no good, let go of the deep-rooted pain I had been harboring for years and let go of situations I could no longer control.

After I finally let go, things began to move, and my life seemed so much better than the days before. Could it have been that simple? I could see the sun again and began opening myself up to new opportunities and adventures. I was hungry for more of what God promised to me. It was then that I reconnected with my old friend's Passion, Purpose, and Power and began to re-image a life that was beautiful and perfectly designed just for me.

Believing that I was not the only one who had almost succumb to their inhibitions, I started pouring and sowing into the lives of women that I knew needed me the most. I began speaking life back into women who were broken, women who had lost faith, women who had become discouraged and women who sought to see their way clear of the circumstances, challenges, and obstacles that hindered their personal and professional growth. Like I once did for myself, I carefully helped them to re-write their stories, re-craft their ambitions, re-direct their energy and re-align themselves with passion, purpose, and power.

And, with each woman I touched and saved from the brink of their destruction, I felt even more compelled to share my story - my story of how an ordinary woman, who had ordinary dreams and who was so desperately broken was able to do the extraordinary by repositioning herself for greatness.

While everybody's story of greatness will undoubtedly be different, this book was birthed out of love for all women who have experienced and are experiencing bouts of brokenness. It was written for women who desire to rise and start living their best life today. Because just like me, at some point in your life, you will have to make the conscious decision to permanently let go of your past, stop worrying about your future and start living in your present.

Understanding that for some, the task of following your passions, surrendering to your purpose and harnessing your power will not be easy, the contents of this book is designed to give you a roadmap to see your way through to your breakthrough. I challenge you to read this book with an open mind and heart and work through the strategies with patience, resilience and the courage needed to make some significant life changes today.

In this book, you will be introduced to my three friends - Purpose, Passion, and Power. I charge you to visualize yourself as these three women, embodying their personalities, attitudes, and emotions. But please understand that you cannot have one without the other. They are a package deal. By personifying them, you will be able to identify with and understand the vital role that each of these concepts plays in your life. In fact, you will be able to see that you might already know them well and have a direct relationship with them.

But before you meet my three friends, I take you on a quest for the discovery of the true meaning and difference between a friendship and a relationship. And, while they are uniquely different, I do this so you can see that they both serve a divine and predestined purpose in your life. And, your relationships and friendships with Passion, Purpose, and Power will be no different. It is your understanding of a friendship and relationship that will help you benefit from your experiences with them. And, that same understanding will help you to connect with them like you never have before or find them if you have yet to encounter them.

Allow the content of these pages to edify your spirit so that you will be prepared to do the work. Your pathway to self - efficacy begins with the turn of this page.

CHAPTER 1

All Friendships Serve a Purpose!

"Even friendships should be weighted in light of our purpose. Be careful of old friends, especially when you have made massive life changes."

—Bishop T.D Jakes

My nana, known for her unrelenting wit and charm, always advised me to keep my enemies close, while I kept my friends just a little closer. It was a proverb that would eventually be proved true. My momma, on the other hand, was the one who told me that if I lay down with dogs, I'd get up with flees—a suggestive phrase that I was more than happy to comply with. Besides, the mere thought of laying down with dogs alone was enough to steer me clear of those who even appeared to be less than worthy of my friendship, much less my love.

Despite their varying perspectives on friendship and relationship-building, their practical advice meant very little to me as a young adult. After all, I was my own woman, and I was more than capable of making my own sound decisions about the people I wished to befriend, particularly those I truly favored. However, the truth remained that I dared not go against the sentiments of my mother or my nana regarding the strangers whom I'd eventually meet. Like most women my age, I was unsure about the people I met. More so, I was uncertain about their intentions with me. In spite of being a social butterfly, I was not too fond of hanging around too many people. In fact, I always opted for a more intimate circle of associates, some of whom have turned out to become very good friends of mine along the way. The irony is that some of those friendships have turned into love interests, some have remained less than desirable as they were before; while others simply dwindled out and died. And for those I lost along the way, I'm grateful for the time we shared together. There are some I wish I had never entertained in the first place, and some I wanted to hold on to forever. After several rounds of this going back and forth, I realized that everyone that comes into your life, friend or foe, is there to serve some purpose, even if you had not summoned them there. Perhaps, each of them had something to teach me.

In addition to letting you learn more about people, friendships have a very peculiar way of teaching you quite a lot about yourself. However, you are cautioned that what you learn might not be what you expected. In developing friendships, you begin to acknowledge the things you like about yourself as well as the things you don't. Friendships also make you aware of the things that you wish you were. From every person I encountered, I learned such a great deal about myself that I almost did not recognize the woman I had become along the way. Friendships have their way of driving you to do the unthinkable, say the unspeakable, and embark upon journeys, alone or with others, that you would not have taken otherwise. In some strange way, good friendships give you strength when you need it, while, simultaneously, bad ones take your power if you let them.

During the course of my life, I've had the pleasure of being acquainted with some pretty dynamic women; women who, in their own right, were brazen with luster, strong, and confident. Some of these women taught me how to be strong, while others brought me to the brink of my own brokenness. Some taught me how to live my life to the fullest, while others tried their best to destroy me. Some taught me how to win, while others tried hardest to defeat me. Some even taught me how to love, while others brought me nothing but fear, grief, and pain. Despite all these relationships and interactions, I find solace in knowing that they all served to teach me valuable lessons about who I was and what I would become.

While, surely, there were many, there are only three who actually remain today. Even though I did not recognize it then, they were all to become constants in my life, permanent fixtures in my present life. They had become my best friends. They are my dynamic trio. Together, we are complete. These ladies have always been there for me when no one else was around. They have all played their roles very well and have helped me through some pretty tough times. And each of them, within their own right, has played, and continues to play, a very important role in my life. We may not always agree, nor do we see eye to eye regarding somethings, but, we always find a way to mesh out our different personalities for the benefit of each other.

Despite the greatness that each of my friends bring, if you are inclined to think that friendships are relationships, I would like to provide you with some clarity on this matter. Some have argued that friendships are merely elaborated relationships, and relationships are nothing more than friendships that are formed as a result of sharing some type of internal bond. But however you try to define them, friendships are very much like a box of chocolates: "*you never know what you are going to get*" until you bite into it and let the contents flow out. Some of them might be soft in the center, cream-filled and sweet, while others may be rough in texture, dark and almost fermented. Some may be salty to taste, while others could be bitter or sour. Despite all the tastes your palate can stand, you should always consider the consequences of indulging in too many sweets. So, before I introduce you to my three friends, it's important for you to understand what friendship really means. It is that what we will explore over course of the next few pages.

Discovering the Purpose in Friendship

If you look back at whatever has transpired in your life, you would realize that there are a some things that you will never be able to forget. Through this process of self reflection, you'd come to the conclusion that while there are some things you'd do over and over again, there exist others you'd surely want to bury forever. Many people will never forget the first person they ever kissed or the person whom they first fell in love with. Some may never forget the first person they ever made love to or the first person who broke their hearts. They will also be people who will never forget the first person against whom they fought or the first person who came into their life as a "friend".

Like many of us, my quest for the purpose of friendship began when I was just a child. The kids I sat with in my kindergarten class, the round-a-way girls I played double-dutch and hopscotch with, and the neighborhood boys I'd race in the streets all served a purpose. At that time, the purpose was association and to merely have fun. Back then, life was easy, and nothing was out of reach. Everyone knew my name, and I was just happy to be a part of the crowd. While I did not realize it then, I would say that these childhood experiences played a role in fostering a certain growth in me that would take me well into my adulthood. They prepared me to face the many challenges that life would throw at me and helped me learn the art of communication, argument, negotiation, and compromise. Most importantly, it taught me how to forgive. So in fact, their presence in my life had served the purpose. These friendships helped to build me, shape me, mold me, and make me, ultimately, defining who and what I would become. They shaped my thinking, gave me reassurance, and helped me to evaluate my character, my flaws and my faith.

To elaborate on just how simplistic my thought process about friendship was and how my experiences with childhood friendships shaped my feelings towards myself, for the sake of argument, we'll call her Tanisha. Tanisha was as beautiful and dignified as they come. She was well-spoken and seemingly mature for her age. And more importantly, I was happy to call her friend. Tanisha was everything I wasn't. She embodied everything I thought I wanted to be. However, by no stretch of the imagination was I ever jealous of her. I was impressed by her eloquence and grace. I mimicked her every move. Dressed the way she dressed, and attempted to wear my hair the way she wore hers. Despite my love for Tanisha, she did very little to boost my self esteem. My infatuation with her alone was not good enough to explain the reasons why I thought that I had to be just like her. Once I had come to those conclusions, had I just discovered the purpose in our friendship? Was she there to teach me something about myself that I had yet to uncover?

Friendships, despite the way they may come or the pain and pleasure they might bring, generally will serve one or more purposes in our lives. The purpose of some friendships is to get us what we want at a particular moment in time. Others are designed to teach us valuable life, character- or career-related lessons. Some friendships come to restore, bringing balance and happiness back into your life, while some come to destroy. While it is true that some friendships are ignited by pure passion, others are perpetuated by the experiences, circumstances, and situations that we've found or put ourselves in.

We form friendships because we are forced to. We form friendships because it's convenient. We form friendships either because they help us to evolve or to have some personal gain. And, we form friendships because we think we're in love or desire to be in love. Despite where or how your friendships are formed, how long they survive, and the outcome they produce, there is a purpose in having met that person. If you would like to put this theory to the test, think about the number of friends you have made over the last twelve months. What was the nature of these friendships? How did they come about? Where were you in your life when you got acquainted with your so-called friend(s)? Despite the answers, the following six clue questions will help you discover the purpose of your friendships.

1. **HAVE YOU RATIONALIZED YOUR OWN NEEDS AND WANTS?**

   Before getting into a friendship, it's always important to rationalize your own needs and wants. Don't be confused by what you want and what you need in friendships. Use your rational thought process to see what is real. More importantly, use it to clearly understand whether your needs and wants are being met in the relationship. There is nothing worse than being in a friendship with someone who does not meet your requirements or refuses to give you some of what you need or want from them.

2. **DO YOU CLEARLY UNDERSTAND THE INTENT?**

   There is a reason behind everything, and everything has a reason. Understanding the intent of your friendships will ensure that you are positioned to embrace the challenges, obstacles, and opportunities that may present themselves along the way.

3. **ARE YOU LISTENING MORE AND TALKING LESS?**

Miscommunication, or the lack thereof, leads to the downfall of many friendships. However, talking too much and not listening for an understanding to take place can be detrimental to your friendships. You must listen intently to understand your friend so that you are able to agree to disagree or kiss and make up. I think we all can agree that the making up part is the best outcome in this scenario.

4. **HAVE YOU BROUGHT IN YOUR SPIRIT OF DISCERNMENT?**

   Discernment can be a powerful tool if you use it correctly. It will help you make sound decisions about your friendships before you even come to the point of making or turning them into full blown relationships. But, more importantly, it will help you to discover the truth in your own direction, understanding and judgments.

5. **HAVE YOU ASKED, OR ARE YOU ASKING THE RIGHT QUESTIONS?**

   Asking the right questions will position you to set the boundaries of your friendships. Taking into the consideration that everyone does not communicate in the same way, don't be afraid to ask for clarity in your friendships. Clarity is nothing more than the picture you see on the wall. Some might see an abstract figure in a painting by Picasso, while some may actually see the women he had chosen to paint.

6. **ARE YOU BEING HONEST AND OPEN?**
   It is always a best practice to seek to be honest and open when deciding on the friendships that you build. As the age old saying goes, "honesty is the best policy" when it comes to making, building, and surviving through the ups and downs of friendships.

Friendships that Turn into Relationships

I have had some great success in turning friendships into full blown relationships. However, when things did not go quite so well, the end result was normally explosive and often times earth-shattering. The best analogy to explain this is witnessing a fire ignite. Friendships that turn into relationships can be much like pouring gasoline on a swelling flame or opening a door or window in a burning building. The danger of opening a window or a door in a burning building is not the fire itself, but the back draft you will encounter as a result.

Admittedly, it was dating that opened my eyes to understanding the importance of friendships. I used to be an eager and tenacious young lady, ready to take over the world, which included, but was not limited to, closely aligning my needs and wants with that of others in every relationship that I had. Unfortunately, like most women of my age back then, my judgment was skewed, and I sacrificed my reality for their perceptions of me and for some their fantasies. Eager to please, I forwent my better judgment, and, ultimately, it was my feelings, needs, and wants that took the back seat to others.

Brian was a high school sweetheart. He was a hunk of a man, and we dated off and on throughout our time in the high school. He was everything to and for me, and our friendship was beyond magical. Before I could think something, he would say it, and before I could ask a question, he would already know the answers. However, our friendship took a different turn when I caught Brian with another girl, a girl I actually despised. He had been telling her all the things he had once told me, and my position in his life became just another story he'd tell his friends during his locker room trash talks. He had hurt me so deep that I thought I'd never be able to love again. However, I soon realized that it was not him that I needed to forgive, it was me. I had allowed him and given him the opportunity to almost destroy me. While I questioned the purpose for all the hurt, it was the pain that explained the reason. I needed to experience such a disaster of a friendship to know what a good one was.

A Friendship and a Relationship Are Not Identical Twins

It's always fascinating to me to hear people say that they are in a relationship with their best friend. However, what most people fail to realize is that friendships and relationships are designed to be mutually beneficial, not mutually exclusive. Friendships are merely relationships that can turn into partnerships. But don't get it twisted; a friendship is not the identical twin to a relationship, since they serve two totally different purposes. Some tend to think that because you are friends with someone, it automatically means that you are in some sort of relationship with them, either spoken or unspoken.

Unlike a friendship, a relationship indicates that there is a connection between two people. More specifically, it implies that an agreement, spoken, written, or implied, has been made between two people who have willfully chosen to come together as one, inadvertently partnering in love, life, or some other affiliation. Relationships are purposefully designed to be binding, unbreakable, and withstanding, similar to that of a parent's relationship to their children or a wife's commitment to her husband and vice versa. But the irony here is that we all know that some parent's relationships with their children are scarred and that some marriages end in divorce.

So, below are some tips that will help you re-evaluate and discern whether you are in a friendship or a relationship.

1. Both friendships and relationships have clear expectations of give and take. It's called reciprocity. Reciprocity refers to a mutual exchange of something that benefits both the parties involved. If you are giving more than you are receiving, chances are you are dealing with someone who is selfish and self-centered. You are not in a relationship, nor are you in a friendship, if you are continually giving more of yourself than others are giving to you.

2. It is true that relationships can be hard, but that is only because they go far beyond admiration and love. They are life-changing and dynamic in nature. They touch

every sense (emotional, physical, spiritual, and psychological) that you'll ever have. If you find that you are consumed by any one of these emotions (fear, anger, rage, happiness, surprise or joy), chances are that you are in a relationship despite the title you have placed on it. On the other hand, friendships, while being driven by emotions, do not play heavily on either one of these emotions. It is a bond or attachment that you share with someone because of affinity, understanding, or a link that you might have with them. Generally speaking, a friendship should not require you to give up who or what you are. Friendships should be complementary, and they should never be bound by any conditions that you set for yourself or for others.

3. True friendships do not have an expiration date. If you find that you have a friendship with someone, which goes off and on again, then chances are that it is not a true friendship. True friendship is unconditional despite the circumstances, and it is not separated by distance or by time. Friendships are designed to support, heal, develop, and enable growth in you.

The Magic in Their Coexistence

Like a bee needs honey, and a moth is attracted to a flame, a friendship needs a relationship as much as a relationship needs an element of friendship. Can you imagine the detrimental effect that would ensue if you were in a relationship where you shared no friendship, a practice that most people engage in?

Some may argue that a relationship necessitates friendship more than a friendship needs a relationship, and that, perhaps, they are even one and the same. But, where many people get it wrong is the inability of people to comprehend that simply because they are in a relationship doesn't mean that they have a friendship. Many relationships have been scarred and broken due to this imbalance and failure of recognizing that their relationship cannot exist without friendship. While they are not identical twins, they need each other to coexist.

Some helpful tips on how to reconcile the coexistence between friendships and relationships are given below:

1. Have you ever heard of anyone having a friendship, much less a relationship, all by themselves? Both a relationship and a friendship require the participation, whether positive or negative, from *two or more* people to either make them work or end them. While I'm sure that it might be possible, it's very difficult to have a friendship or a relationship all by yourself.

2. Slightly differing in the degree of intensity is that every friendship and relationship is *bound by a set of expectations.* These expectations can be shared by either party involved or be mutually exclusive to only one. Nonetheless, the boundaries of expectations in both a relationship and a friendship

will set the stage for the many interactions you will have with each other.

3. Relationships and friendships will always share the same outcome. They begin *purposefully* or *unintentionally*, and while some may last, others will wither away with time. While there are generally no expectations pertaining to the longevity of either one of them, they both will surely come to an end.

4. If you are in either, you need to determine whether it is serving its true purpose for you, since both a friendship and a relationship are *designed to make you grow*. If you are not growing in your friendships or relationships, you must make a conscious decision to pull yourself out of it and let them go. This may include ending abusive or tremulous marriages, breaking connections with spirit breakers and dream robbers, or even cutting ties with your long-standing besties. In a perfect world, friendships will always turn into full blown relationships. In fact, it is the ideal recipe for a blissful, harmonious, and healthy life. However, understanding the role that friendships and relationships play in your life is of utmost importance while making decisions about the people who you allow to enter in your life and the ones you need to let go. A deep understanding of their intent is warranted to fully embrace the many benefits they will bring or the subsequent

challenges you will experience with them. As with all relationships and friendships alike, they all serve a purpose.

Now, let me briefly introduce you to my three friends.

PART I

MEET THE GIRLS

AN UNLIKELY ALLIANCE

"Oh my God, my girlfriends are everything to me. They celebrate with you; they cry with you, they hold you when you need to be held. They laugh with you. They're mean with you! They're always there, and it's just a priceless thing to have."

—Jennifer Lopez

CHAPTER 2

Meet Passion

I'm so fly...that Ride or Die Kinda Chic

I met my dear old friend, Passion, when I was only five years old, playing in a schoolhouse yard. Passion is a person whom one would call a disruptive individual—a wild child. She is a childhood friend of mine, and she has been a part of my life since the very beginning. She is, as she was back then, driven and motivated, enchanting and rambunctious. She is more than loud, but her charisma lets her carry that with ease. Oftentimes, she is overbearing with her senseless ambiguity and her lack of direction and focus. And, I'm sure that we all know people just like that! You know those people, the ones who are emotionally-driven creatures and who will get excited or angered at the drop of a dime. Yeah, that's my friend Passion!

She is charming and enduring, yet she is confident and bold. She indulges in taking risks, however, she likes to keep her risks calculated. And, she's more than willing to try anything more than once, while doing what she wants and whenever she wants to do it, without having much regard or regret for the consequences that would ensue. She's driven and thrifty, strong, and oftentimes uncontrollable. She's a "no holds bars", my ride or die kind of chic. Everybody loves her. Everybody wants to be her. And, everybody wants to date her. But, they do not know or understand how to initially embrace her. My friend and I, we are thick as thieves, and she motivates and pushes me more than anything or anyone whom I've ever encountered. She is the last person I talk to at night and the first person I call upon when I wake up.

She is the person I share my hopes and dreams with, and she is the first person to say "*Shame on you for not believing*". We've shared so many good times that the bad times don't seem to mean very much. While we do not always get it right, we fight it out until we come to a resolution. She's never steered me in the wrong direction. However, I must admit that her tendency to over reach is far from being perfect and is downright quite annoying.

She is the one I go on adventures with, and the one who attempts to make all the rules. But, I must admit that I like the fact that she is the dreamer and the one who stirs up the confidence in me to seek after my hearts desires. She always makes me smile, and she loves to be at the center of attention, even if she is only entertaining herself. Passion makes me anxious to complete tasks or start a new one. I dare not shut her down or shut her up. Doing so only makes her more excited and eager to get things done. She has no limits and takes pleasure in pushing the boundaries of our friendship. But, I love her just the same.

Passion is always the one trying to make a dollar out of fifteen cents. She is definitely the one who can surely turn a quarter, nickel, or dime into a dollar. She is just so innovative like that. I remember calling on Passion to help me understand

and plan out my next big move. While she was no good at helping me plan it out, she served up a nice "*can of inspiration and stomp it out!*" Our friendship feels almost like a curse because while I know that I love and need her, oftentimes, I am left in limbo by her, scouring to find truth and direction. She tries to make you think that you must balance your practicality to save face with your ambitions.

This girl always has something up her sleeves, and she always finds a way to pull me right into her unyielding grasps. She is so forward thinking and impatient that she sometimes forgets that what she might actually need is directly in front of her. Without any question or hesitation, she feels that everything she is compelled to do must be accomplished and achieved. She will go to the ends of the earth to make sure that things are done, oftentimes forgetting that it takes time to watch your dreams and visions grow.

In many ways, Passion and I are very much alike. We enjoy our freedom to dream and dream big - even when everybody around us doubts our anticipated outcomes. She take the place of many of the friends in my life when I am uncertain about my next move. I am there for her as she was for me when I quit my job and launched my first successful business. She was the one whispering in my ear that I can make it and would ultimately push me to keep going when the road ahead became bumpy. She is that gentle reminder of what life would be like without her presence in my life.

Her relationships outside of our immediate circle took a toll on both her personal and professional life. They have quite frequently left her in despair, searching for truth. While she enjoyed her relationships with success, perfection and even love, she runs from friendships with fear, rejection and pain. After all these years of knowing her, I still cannot figure her out. She's a complex individual, with a mind that some might call genius. The reality is that all she ever wants is to be fulfilled and to live the very best life that she can live.

CHAPTER 3

Meet Purpose

Savory to the Touch, yet Sassy and Sweet

Purpose is sassy, unlike my friend Passion, mixed with a little sweetness. She is cool, calm, and collected—a mellow and pretty kind of girl. She is the whole truth and nothing but the truth. She is suave and sleek, sincere and endearing, and far from superficial. She's that around the away girl with that sex appeal - physicality, emotionality, and intellect - that all the girls envy. She is majestic in her walk and smooth in her talk. She never falters, but she fades in an out like a dream during restless sleep. This girl, my girl, is soft to the core and never rough around the edges, setting her stamp on everyone she encounters.

However, she and I were never really that close, as she did not come into my life until my mid 20's. Truth be told, when I first met her, I didn't quite like her. In fact, she got under my skin. She, somehow, changed the game for Passion and me, and we were hardly thrilled with what we thought her intentions where. I'm not quite sure why, but she was always very hard to figure out, almost borderline standoffish and distant. Yet, she was poised and positioned, unwavering and very passive. Everything she said seemed to make sense, and her words had the tendency to cut through you like a knife. Her mere presence amidst our inner circle made our daily encounters with her almost uncomfortable, since Passion and I were used to hanging ourselves out on multiple limbs; after all, Passion and I were both dreamers.

Despite all odds, Passion and I gave her a chance to prove that she was worthy of a spot on our team. Our dynamic duo had turned into a trio. Despite her mystery, she was admirable and reasonable. But, she stood steadfast was not easily influenced. She would often standby and watch Passion and me run amuck and do the things we probably should not have been doing. And, while she was not an "*I told you so*" kind of person, you clearly understood her position when it came to certain things, in fact, all things.

Many people describe Purpose as the girl with the master plan, the girl who is always striving and reaching. She delicately took her spot as the strategic artist in our group. Despite what we thought her shortcomings were, she showed us how inviting she could really be. She kept us focused and thoughtful, concise and always deliberate. She stirred up the greatness in us and helped us push through pain. She was the one who told us that "*When one door closes, another one would open*", and she urged us to dream with our eyes wide open. She is the one who took over the rope when it became too short to handle and provided us with more length to carry on with our journeys. She was the voice of reason—the one who did nothing without first making sure that all paths were clear.

My friend Purpose is what you call an "Action Jackson". She creates the space and opportunity for Passion and me to operate. Now that I think of it, Purpose is the reason that Passion and I were so happy in the first place. While we did not recognize it then, it was Purpose who had been setting us up for what was to come over the next few years. Purpose made us realize that without each other, we were nothing more than just that dynamic duo—those dream-chasers we often referred to ourselves as. Having Purpose in the picture and a part of our clique, we were no longer bound by the limitations of our imagination, but we were positioned to accept our destinies.

CHAPTER 4

Meet Power

Bad and Boojee, the Bomb.com

More than being bad and boojee, my girl Power is no joke. She is the "*bomb.com*" and everything in between. She's whom you would refer to as a seasoned kind of girl—slightly intimidating and rough around the edges. She's the type of girl you'd take to a fight, not hoping that she'd win but knowing that she'd win. She is borderline crazy and has a quirky sense of humor. She is deliberate, and she is more than competent, strong, and wise. She is the dominant figure in our clique, and her strength can be perceived from miles away.

She is raw, talented, and aggressive, yet she is very result-oriented. Her mere presence in a room is endearing. Everyone knows that she is there without her even having to open her mouth. She is polished and professional. Yet, she is candid and full of grit. She walks with grace as if she was a queen, and her distinctive aura is alluring and breathtaking.

Power joined our clique by accident. In fact, I was introduced to her by Purpose. And, as if we needed any help, Purpose felt that Power would be a great addition to our already-strong sisterhood. Purpose insisted that she'd be the perfect match to balance us all out. But, boy, was Purpose wrong! That's, at least, what we thought. I still wonder to this day what she might have been thinking, and, better yet, where did Power come from? After all, I had never seen the likes of her kind. However, her angelic, yet devilish, ambiance sparked our curiosities.

Power's presence only complicated things, and she was not easily received by Passion and me. In fact, we tried to dismiss her by ignoring every attempt she made to infiltrate our clique. But, she somehow managed to make room for herself in our inner circle, subtly taking us all by force. Her sheer nerve was nauseating, but, nonetheless, we went along with the recommendation of Purpose and accepted her as one of our own.

In the beginning of our friendship, Power remained a very silent figure. In fact, she rarely reared her face or showed up for any of our life events. We had no idea what we were in for and if, in fact, she would ever release her full force. However, three years into our friendship, she began to show her true colors—colors that were perfectly matched with her disposition and her personality.

This is when we learned that Power had split personalities, and it was frightening to say the least. In one moment, she was this bold, fearless being, and, in the next, she was a pussy cat waiting to be stroked by the egos of those who surrounded her. Little did we know that this was a pungent tactic to command the attention of her unsuspecting prey. She reels you in with her charm and wit, and then, without warning or notice, she releases a captivating stronghold on you. Trust me when I tell you, for I've witnessed it firsthand. Many have fallen victim to

Power's sensual tendencies, only to be left speechless and wanting more.

Purpose's disposition was well aligned with that of Power. But, Power and Purpose often bumped heads, despite their affinity towards each other. In spite of sharing many of the same qualities, they chose to display them in different ways. To add insult to injury, Purpose and Power would go months without even speaking or connecting with each other. The more Power tried to show up, the more Purpose tried to shut her out. I never quite understood why this was the case, considering that it was Purpose who made her introduction.

Power was of the mind-set to take things by force and do it with rigor and accuracy, while Passion was more agile in her decision making and stance. Power made us believe that there was no one better than us and that we were in a position to take over the world, sometimes even in the midst of our brokenness. The actions she took were risky, and the things she did only confirmed what we had been thinking all along—either this woman was downright crazy (insane might be a better word), or there might have been some reason behind her madness.

Our uncertainty pertaining to Power's reactions to many things took a toll on our growing friendship. She was too erratic and unpredictable. She could also be quite unforgiving at times. Her judgment often seemed skewed. But, somehow, we were all pleased at her efforts and the outcomes that she achieved. She had this way of manifesting things out of nothing and creating nothing out of something. Most of all, her ability to make even the least likely of believers believe made her appealing. I guess you can say that she just had that magic touch—a touch that I could have only hoped to have one day. A part of me envied her, while the other part feared her, never knowing when she would pull her thunder out on me or those around us.

Unlike Passion and Purpose, I tried hard to make it work with Power. Besides, how much did I really have to lose? Power was slowly beginning to grow on me, and everything she did and said became admirable. She was indirectly forming an alliance with me as she possessed characteristics that neither Passion or Purpose or even I, for that matter, possessed. She made me feel strong when I was weak, and she forced me to make moves that I would have never tried to make. She had this knack of pushing me out of my comfort zone and made me begin to play roles that I thought I was not prepared to take.

Despite all this, as I became more familiar and comfortable with her tendencies, I soon began to let her in slowly. With hesitation, I embraced her with half-open arms and prepared myself for the storms that I knew she would inadvertently create in my life. However, I held onto her like a crack head on dope, feening for my next fix.

Unlike Passion and Purpose, Power introduced me to an outer body experience, an experience that is more than difficult to describe. She was like a one-night stand, often times leaving me at the front door without even kissing me goodbye.

While it was Passion that drove me to embellish my visions and my dreams, it was Power that took over when it was time for me to take the center stage. She filled me with such anxiety that I was anchored to her like a ship in shallow waters. I wanted to know more. I needed to know more. I was totally enthralled with her disposition and wit.

Over the next few years, our friendship really began to grow deeper. In fact, it blossomed into something much more majestic. While we had our ups and downs, I began spending more time with her, more than I ever did with Passion and Purpose.

PART II

A PATHWAY TO EFFICACY

STEER YOUR WAY CLEAR

"Sometimes you've got to let everything go - purge yourself. If you are unhappy with anything...whatever is bringing you down, get rid of it. Because you'll find that when you're free, your true creativity, your true self comes out."

—Tina Turner

CHAPTER 5

Following Passion

"Passion is energy. Feel the power that comes from focusing on what excites you."

—Oprah Winfrey

When I was a child, I was filled with a lot of hope and, what some called, promise. I believed that anything was possible, and my young and impressionable mind ran wild at the thoughts of what my adult life would be. Like most kids my age, I dreamt of the becoming something truly magical. While I could not pin point what that magical something was, I was certain that I was destined for something so much bigger than myself. Filled with so much gumption and tenacity, I yearned for the day when I would take my rightful place amongst the elite, exhibiting my skills, talents, and abilities to all who'd dare to watch. My passions ran very deep since I was an enthusiast about everything that I loved. Now that I think of it in hindsight, I loved a lot of things.

However, my one true passion was and still remain my love for music. It was music that somehow always filled my soul. It gave me a strange sort of energy—one that I had never felt before. It comforted me when I was sad, healed me when I was angry, and brought me joy when I was happy. As a result, I joined my high school chorus and sung every Sunday in the church choir. I took piano and voice lessons at the Newark Community School of the Arts. I even learned how to play the drums.

I recall being so very nervous during my first real performance, that it was downright nauseating. I was shaking like a leaf, my mouth became dry, and I felt dizzy—all at the same time. But, I stood on that stage facing the audience with my head held high and my chest poked out, simply proud to have the opportunity to do what I loved at that moment. As the audience looked on, I belted out a soft and even toned "I Believe the Children are Our Future", the first line in Whitney Houston's Grammy award winning song, 'Greatest Love of All'.

From that moment on, I would sing to and for anyone who cared to listen. I would listen to music upon waking up and close my eyes to it upon going to sleep. I would listen to music while going to school as well as while coming back, and I'd sing and listen to it in the shower and around the house. I was mesmerized by the sharpness of the soprano tone, the mellow sounds of the alto, and the highs and lows of the tenors. I enjoyed all types of music. Be it group bands or solo artists singing and playing rhythm and blues, old time funk or gospel music, I loved them all. While I no longer sing or play as much as I'd like to, my love and passion for music has never faded even though it has not become my ultimate career choice. I continue to do the things that I did as a child to cultivate and nurture this passion for music, without the front and center stage performances that is.

Shaped by my life experiences, it wasn't until I became much older that I began to envision doing the impossible, conquering all my most deeply rooted fears, even those I didn't know existed, to live the best life possible. I had become accustomed to walking in my own truth, harnessing every opportunity that was afforded to me while using life's challenges as the propeller to achieve my goals and my dreams.

By the time I had become an adult, I had officially run out of fingers counting the many times I heard, "Dang girl! You just started another new business? What else are you going to do?" or "Can't you just focus on one thing? Why do you need to do this right now?" And, I've even heard "If you like it, I love it". I'm still not too sure what the last one meant, but these were the words that were spoken by the many people whom I've encountered along the way. These are the words spoken by individuals who had no earthly clue as to what it meant to have Passion as a friend. I followed her around like a puppy on a leash; she guided my every step and proctored my every move. And, I let her because, admittedly, I loved her and the way she made me feel.

Despite my feelings towards Passion, not too many people saw her in the same way. As a child, she was cute. However, as an adult, she was a torn in my side, unmistakably the error that caused, as some would say, all of my problems. The closer I followed Passion, the further away my relationship with others became. For the people around me, specifically, the ones who said that they loved me, she became a nuisance because she took away the time I would spend with them. Perhaps there was some validity to their feelings, but this only made me want to pursue her even more feverishly and fearlessly.

Then, there were those who claimed to understand my relationship with Passion. Some even went as far to say that they supported it and endorsed it. However, all the while, they selfishly wished for our defeat. These were the ones who told me that my journey in following Passion made me too strong, and I needed to downplay my position to be of any value to others. The irony in that frame of thought is that they emphatically claimed to love that part of me, but they could not handle all that came with it. But, here is one thing that they did not know. My journey with Passion is mine and mine alone. It is not for the benefit of others but for the fulfillment of myself.

The lesson for those who are following Passion is to keep on in your journey with Passion despite who or what might try to sow doubt, confusion, curves, and bends along your way. Your journey with Passion is specific to your desires and dreams, and it should not be interrupted by the inhibitions and insecurities of others. In doing so, it is very important that you lean on your relationship with Passion to help drive you forward. Do not give up so much of who you are to make others feel comfortable about your relationship with them.

Passion Defined

As with many other things, there are varying perspectives with regard to who and what Passion is. Some tend to believe that passion is having the courage to face your fears, embrace the impossible, and walk with confidence. Others believe that passion is the excitement that you feel towards your convictions, opinions, and thoughts. A more formal definition of passion surmises that it is an intense feeling or desire for something or someone. For example, the infinite amount of love that you might have had towards your first love. However, a more fascinating perspective of passion can be found in the descriptions of those who believe that passion is what drives short-and long-term success. In essence, it is the actions behind your dreams, visions, and goals that constitute passion—the very same passion that I had for music as a child.

Despite these varying perspectives, if one is to put it simply, passion is that thing inside of you that drives your everyday life. Passion will make you buy a new car when your old one is running just fine. Passion will make you start a new business venture when you are not emotionally, physically, or financially prepared for such an undertaking. Passion will make you take risks, when the risks of doing something outweigh its potential benefits. Passion will make you take a stance on an issue that you do not fully understand, and Passion will make you believe that you are unstoppable when you are not yet strong enough, to handle the bumps and bruises that you'll encounter along the way, and I do mean that literally. She is the one who holds the master key to your dreams and your heart's desires. And, even though she does not own it, she is the gatekeeper of your existence, and she prides herself in the mastery of her own ambitions.

Passion will give you courage and help you to position yourself to be the leader you naturally are. She will keep you balanced and, more importantly, always positioned for greatness. Passion will help you run circles around your adversaries and help you to step up and address the inconsistencies in your life. She will emphatically help in restoring your stamina and help you to realize your purpose. Since Passion is not only limited to your personal life, Passion must be seen as the conduit for everything that you will encounter. People should see her in your walk, hear her in your talk, and feel her in your presence.

This may sound contradictory to what has been mentioned before, because having Passion as a friend sounds like a very good thing, right? Of course, having Passion is a good thing. But, it's important to note that passion is not a requirement for all things in your life. It is not a requirement for love, because you can surely love someone and not be passionate about them. Have you ever been in a relationship with someone and soon realized that you did not share the same intense feelings towards them as they did for you? Similarly, Passion is not a requirement for some of the professional successes that you might have had or if you are seeking a job or even career satisfaction. Take for instance, you could be really good at what you do for work or in your career, and, in fact, you could really enjoy what you do. But, that does not mean that you are passionate about it. You merely enjoy it because you do it well and make money while doing it.

I'm not sure when I let her take over completely, but she poured on me like a thunderstorm, setting the path for everything that would happen in my life. She was right there guiding what I thought were my decisions and what I really wanted. She has also been there when I needed her the most.

Isn't it funny how we let someone or something control our every move, making waves in our peaceful existence? But, come to think of it, where would we be without her? After all, she is the one who gives you hope.

While they may never admit it, people spend a lifetime under her spell and would gladly follow her everywhere she goes. Don't get me wrong here. Having Passion in your life is a good thing. However, having too much of a good thing can also be bad. Passion has been known to take out even the strongest of individuals, leaving them feeling defeated and insufficient. Too much Passion for multiple things, all at the same time, guarantees your demise and causes unnecessary frustration and stress that I'm sure you could do without.

While it is certainly okay to be guided by passion, like most things, passion requires focus in order to see itself through. It requires you to prioritize what is most important and makes you aware of the things you should let go of. In order to fully appreciate the benefits of having Passion as a friend, you must learn to let go of things that do not complement the true Passion in your life. This includes, but is not limited to, people, circumstances, and situations. You must also learn how to advance the mission of Passion while providing a buffer for her to thrive and grow, develop and be realized.

In my own assessment of the perspectives on passion, I've concluded that there are some key lessons that are to be embraced. I have summed them up as follows:

- You must **consciously choose** your passions. Choosing your passion(s) is much like choosing your best friend. You must let your heart guide you, using your ambitions and desires to drive your decisions about what you love, what you don't like, what you aspire to be, where you'd like to go, and how you are going to get there.

- You must **breathe life** into your passions in order to make it (them) real. Make your passions real by putting an "*action*" behind them.

- You must **groom, nurture, and protect** your passions. Passions are much like children. In order for them to thrive and grow, they must be groomed, shaped, nurtured, and protected. You must continually work on and through them in order to see the benefits they will afford you.

- You must **align** your passion with your own personal goals of growth and development. If passions are to help you grow and develop as an individual, they are incumbent upon your ability to align them with your own personal goals. Don't allow the passions of others to drive your ambitions. I am oftentimes amazed and shocked at the number of people who forgo their own passions for the sake of others. Allow your passions to live within yourself and don't be afraid to be selfish about what you need.

Passion Almost Killed Me

Despite everything I loved about Passion and what she brought me, she was a dirty ol' girl! On more than one occasion, I felt as if Passion was a curse, a big old monkey on my back. She never let up on me. She even wrestled with me when I was sleep. I can recall the countless restless nights I spent in sitting up and talking to her silently under my voice. No one, apart from me, could see her or hear her. She'd do all the talking. Whenever I tried to get a word in, she'd interrupt what I considered my logical train of thought and thinking. She fed off my emotions, all of my fears, and my pain as well. She even took a bit of my happiness, leaving me feeling empty inside at times. She was that unintentional part of me that would rise up when I least expected her to. True to her characteristics, she was divine. But, I had to learn how I could control her, if not for anything but for my own peace of mind.

Despite the varying perspectives on Passion, I surmise that Passion and your relationship with her is nothing more than a misguided representation of dreams. It is a burning desire to do, accomplish, or have something you've never experienced before. For those who are purely dreamers, Passion can be painfully taunting for the soul, downright earth-shattering, when seemingly you are unable to birth life into those dreams. As a result, many people grow weary of trying, becoming resentful at best, and separate themselves from the vision. While I had a strong relationship with Passion and rarely had any problems reconciling my feelings with her, she would often put me in positions where I would be almost afraid to dream. The feelings would overwhelm me so deeply that I would fall into a catatonic state of depression, becoming paralyzed in deep thought.

Despite her involvement in my life, I've come to learn that Passion requires balance—a balance in both the personal and the professional life. What many people fail to realize is that Passion is merely an emotion that is driven by feelings, such as joy, faith, fear, opportunity, anger among other things. And, it is even driven by rage sometimes. Passion is not concerned about how you are going to get what you want or what you have to go through in order to achieve something. She's only concerned about the present, having very little consideration of the consequences that might ensue.

Passion, Please Don't Die

Since many people do not understand the dynamic nature of Passion, they give up on her when things don't quite go their way or when things seem to go astray. They put her in a dusty closet with every intention of pulling her back out. But, you cannot kill Passion. You simply smother her by losing hope. Many people lose her unintentionally because they are unable to handle the responsibilities of having her. She requires a lot of work. She is much like a new-born baby; Passion requires a tender kind of love, a love that is so unconditional that it's nearly impossible to break.

There are those who would argue that they've lost Passion because they simply had too much on their plates or that they just did not have the support that they needed to work through their challenges or even pain. This could not be farther from the truth. The reality is that many people have succumbed to Passion's grip, choking out before they even realized the Purpose in her existence.

If you are not careful, Passion will keep you on a never-ending rollercoaster, with dips and loops, preparing you for a freefall that may never come. If you want to get off that rollercoaster, stop letting Passion take the keys and drive away in your car. Be the driver of your own ride and use Passion to fuel it up when you are about to hit empty. You'll know when you need refueling since that infamous red light, you know the one that screams "pay me some attention", will come on to alert you that you only have a couple of more miles to go.

Directions for Following Passion

Are you uncertain about where your passion lies? Don't worry. The good news is that passions run deep, and it's highly unlikely that you'll ever find yourself in a position where you've lost them. They can, however, become like dreams deferred if you are unable, unwilling, or unready to actively participate in seeing them come to fruition.

Following your passions is much like following directions. For some, following directions come easily, and they need no particular guidance or assistance with where they are going. They are arbitrarily in tune with the elements and the environment around them. However, there are many others who can't seem to find their way without the assistance of a GPS. Sometimes, they seem to get lost even with the assistance of a GPS. Generally, these are the people who attempt to take shortcuts along the way despite reading the directions given to them.

There are no shortcuts in following Passion. You must follow the directions and take the correct path to reach your ultimate destination. While, surely, there could be several different routes that you can take to reach your destination, some a little shorter or longer than others, the paths are generally not that different from each other. For example, if you are traveling northbound on I95 and decide to take a back road to avoid traffic or toll roads, your GPS will re-route you on an alternate route going in a direction headed north. If you've entered the address correctly, it will not turn you completely around to head back south.

During this process of rerouting, you might notice a slight difference in your new arrival time or the number of extra miles you'll drive that may help you avoid traffic and tolls. But, everything else will remain the same. You will still be heading north. If you are one who requires the utility of assistance, here are your directions for following your passion.

Your Starting Point: Dream with Your Eyes Wide Open

Before my grandmother passed away, I spent a lot of time with her. She was my rock, next to my rock, my support system. We'd spend countless hours talking about my plans for the future and my greatest fears. My grandmother would always offer her words of wisdom, encouraging me to pursue all my wild ideas. We shared a special bond, and our relationship was one of the more constants in my life. When she went home to be with the Lord, I yearned to see her once more, hear her voice and feel her touch. She was the one who'd get me through some very tough times. Notwithstanding, days without her turned into months, and months turned into years, and she had yet to come visit me in my dreams. If only I could get a glimpse of her, and get her to offer some guidance.

My wish would come true four years after her passing. Grandmother came to me in a dream. I was sitting on a large rock that was located right beside what appeared to be a river or a stream. The water was crystal-white, and you could see straight to the bottom. I was mesmerized by the sun's silhouette hitting the surface of the water. I could see my reflection bouncing through the ripples of the water as it went downstream. I pondered about my life, thinking of the things I loved and the things I despised. For the first time in my life, I was lost and felt so broken.

As I was lost in my thoughts, I could see someone walking towards me down the river's bend. Rather than being afraid, I was more curious about who it could be. As the person got closer, I could see her face. I was most surprised to see that it was my grandmother. She perched down on a rock next to mine, placed her hand on my knee, and said, "What's wrong, baby?" With tears rolling down my face, I said, "I'm so confused and lost without you. I desperately need your guidance and love." "Everything is going to be alright," she replied, "Keep on doing what you are doing and don't give up." She kissed me on my forehead and proceeded to leave. But, I called her name and reached out for her hand. She turned back to me and said, "Don't cry, my sweet daughter. Awake now, and dream with your eyes wide open."

I woke up from that dream feeling more inspired than ever before. I got what I needed from her, just when I needed it the most. She not only reaffirmed what I already knew, but she gave me the courage to continue to pursue my dreams.

Turn Right in 12 miles: Take Action on Passion

You must be an active participant in your relationship with Passion. Passion is far from an idle girl. She requires stamina, commitment, and stroking. What many fail to realize is that their relationship with Passion is futile if they are not willing to do the work to actually have a relationship with her. Like anything else you deem worthy of your time, you must find a way to work it out with her, reconciling your faith in her. In an effort to ensure that your relationship is mutually beneficial, you must take action with Passion and not be afraid to strategize your next move with her. We are reminded of this truth in the book of James (2:14–18. NKJV) who said that faith is dead without work.

> [14] What *does it* profit, my brethren, if someone says he has faith but does not have works? Can faith save him?[15] If a brother or sister is naked and destitute of daily food, [16] and one of you says to them, "Depart in peace, be warmed and filled," but you do not give them the things which are needed for the body, what does it profit?[17]Thus, also faith by itself, if it does not have works, is dead.[18]

I like to think of Passion as a contributor to the items on my bucket list because she helps me fill it up. She is the one who inspires me to take the risks and to embrace the opportunities to do, say, and be everything that I want to be. Let me show you just how simple it can be to put faith, dreams, and vision into action.

If you have a burning desire to climb the Rocky Mountains, schedule a hiking adventure that will take you there. You might need to save up some money to make the trip there. But, put down a small deposit to at least hold your spot.

If you have an unyielding desire to dance in the rain, take off your shoes for God's sake and start prancing on the next rainy day. Weather forecasts can be pretty accurate, and they will give you an indication of when you need to be prepared. Make an effort to not take your umbrella out that day.

If you have a gut-wrenching desire to save a broken relationship, call your loved one today, not tomorrow, and make amends. Forget how you feel for just this one moment. Pick up the phone, dial the number (do not hang up), and start your call with a simple hello.

If you have a strong desire to learn how to swim because you love the ocean, take a swimming class to perfect your stroke. Fear is our greatest detractor in our path of doing what we love and what makes us feel good. Start in the baby pool before graduating to the deeper one. Slowly take on your next feat at swimming in the deep water. The hurdle is to just get into the water.

If you desire to have children but, for some reason, are unable to bear them, adopt one or two that need a permanent home. Scout your local foster care system, call an adoption agency, or ask a friend.

If you have a strong desire about leaving a mentally, emotionally, and physically abusive relationship, plan your fastest exit. Stand in the mirror and look at the person that is staring back at you. Tell her that you love her and that you are worth it. Find a support, a trusted friend or family member, and pack your bags and leave when he's gone. The rest will take care of itself.

If you have a burning desire to lose weight and get healthy, get up and go to the gym. If you can't afford a gym membership or don't have time to commit to the charge, walk your way to a healthy life. Commit to walking at least three days a week.

If you have a desire to become financially independent, make a promise to yourself to stop spending, get out of debt, take on a second job, and start saving. Start with a small goal to save just 2% of your weekly earnings. Put that away in your sock drawer or open an interest-bearing savings account. Online banking has made it easy for you to get started.

And, if you have a desire to run your own business, connect with like-minded individuals who can help you achieve that goal. Begin to come out of your shell and start networking with people you've only heard about. Create a new circle of friends and start doing your homework. If you find yourself to be stuck, find a mentor or coach to guide you.

Turn Left in 16 miles: Brace Yourself for the Fall

For those of you who enjoy a great thrill, do you remember the Kingda Ka, El Toro, Nitro, the Dark Night, the Batman and Robin, and the Rolling Thunder roller coasters? I loved the excitement of being strapped onto a harness or a seat and dangling helplessly more than 200 feet in the air, all while spinning and turning through and around hoops and tracks at speeds of up to 80 mph. What a rush!

Understanding that it could be dangerous, many of us who enjoy riding coasters take the risk because we are not really concerned about falling. We take the risk merely for the sheer joy that it brings us in those few minutes in which the coaster is in flight. And, while in flight, we pray to the Gods to keep us safe and to protect us from any harm. Some even utter the words "Lord, please don't let this coaster come off its tracks".

The lesson here is that no one really likes to fall. In fact, it can be downright scary to think about the possibilities of it actually happening. However, the reality of it is that no one is truly really afraid of the fall itself, they are terrified of the impact. As a result, people try and break the fall by putting their hands out, anchoring their legs, or closing their eyes. Some even hold their breath, thinking that it will somehow slow the heart rate down long enough to calm their nerves.

Your relationship with Passion will be much like a roller coaster. Sometimes, she will take you up, while she will have you down at other instances. She will have you all high spirited at one moment and downright confused and afraid in the next. Your job at that time would be to follow her lead, brace for the fall, and simply enjoy the ride.

Destination is on your right in 1.8 miles: Now, Let Go

Your relationship with Passion requires you to let go of your inhibitions, live in the moment, and stretch your imagination beyond what you can see right in front of you. Just like riding that roller coaster in mile marker 16, once you are airborne and that coaster has left the station, there is nothing more you can do but sit back and simply enjoy the ride.

The process of letting go ensures that you are able to enjoy the things in your life that move and drive you. For some, they get pleasure and excitement in learning new things and may have a deep-rooted love for mastery, intuition, intellect, edification, and knowledge. They are passionate, and, therefore, committed to observing and interacting with the phenomena and possibilities of exploration in the world around them. They are drawn to spending their time in this space and find peace and comfort here, much like the case of myself and music. However, in order for people to truly embrace this passion for learning, they must learn to let go of their biases, own thoughts and opinions, and be open to receiving and digesting the perspectives of new ideas and understanding.

I've come to realize through following my own journey with passion that you don't need to sacrifice everything to make the trip. Following your passion is not an "all or nothing" ordeal. Life is not about choosing which dreams to pursue but choosing the ones that will make you the most fulfilled, the ones that will edify your soul and heighten your awareness of purpose, meaning, and accomplishment. But, passion requires focus, some level of clarity, and a commitment to it.

Arguably, some tend to think that having passion is the setup for disappointment, since if you don't do well or fail to achieve or satiate that passion, you will become demotivated and remain stuck in a place of stagnation and, perhaps, even resentment. But, what they fail to tell you is that passion drives ambition, and ambition, no matter how long it takes to discover, drives success. While there are surely some other dynamics at play, even the great minds of the world, past and present, have alluded to passion as the platform to their success.

Steve Jobs – *"People with passion can change the world for the better."*

Jay Z – *"I think it's the passion for what you do … and you finding something that you can be true to … something that's really close to who you are as a person. You have to have PASSION for what you do … I LOVE it."*

Jon Bon Jovi – *"Nothing is as important as passion. No matter what you want to do with your life, be passionate."*

Zig Ziglar – *"Passion is the driving force behind success."*

Tony Robbins – *"Passion is the genesis of genius."*

To further illustrate this important perspective, I would like to present a scenario. Have you ever witnessed a baby learning to walk? Children can teach us many valuable lessons about letting go. When a child first learns to walk, they hold onto their mother's hands, or maybe I should say that the mother holds on to them, afraid that they might hit the ground. However, as the child gets more comfortable with each step that it takes, they slowly pull away from their mother, hoping to take the next step alone. When they have finally let go altogether, the excitement of accomplishing just this small feat is greater than anything they have ever felt before.

Passion dwells in the eye of the beholder, and it can be described as an internal instinct that is a vital part of your survival. If you are unwilling and unable to follow your passions, you must ask yourself the question "What are you living for?" While there are surely many other reasons for living, your passion for something drives you towards making and getting the most out of your life. Passion is an important ingredient to understanding and finding your relationship with Purpose.

CHAPTER 6

Surrendering to Purpose

Purpose isn't Purpose unless it's Purposeful…

"It's not enough to have lived. We should be determined to live for something."

—Winston S. Churchill

"Girl, I think I am finally done finding my life's Purpose" is the most common ideology shared by those who have come to reason with and accept the many setups and setbacks in their journey of life. You know, those kinds of setbacks that almost knocked you to your feet or shook you so hard that you feared not being able to ever get back up. Or, what about those setups that looked promising but were doomed with failure from the very start? If you are one of them, I challenge you to ask yourself the question "Have I really found my life's Purpose, or am I merely following my dear ole friend Passion?"

To illustrate just how confused I was, I had managed to rack up more than twenty so-called Purposes for my life over the span of 20 years. Every year, and with every new undertaking, I had found a new Purpose. When I graduated from undergraduate school and pursued doctoral studies, I had found a purpose. When I met and married my husband, I had found another purpose. When I became a mother, I found a different purpose. After quitting my job and launching my first successful business, I had found yet another purpose. Later when I became an educator, I had found a new purpose. Becoming a motivational speaker, I found a newer purpose. And, with every new social or professional organization I would join or affiliate myself with, I would find a new purpose. In hindsight, how many purposes could one person actually have had?

Purpose's antics were so convincing that even the people around me thought that I had actually found my life's purpose. However, in reality, Purpose was yet to find me.

Purpose, Who Art Thou?

Understanding who and what Purpose is, is the first step towards being a happier and healthier version of yourself. Great scholars, spiritual advisors, and professionals have all taken a stab at helping us to understand the connections that Purpose has in our lives. Let's briefly examine a few of those perspectives.

Bishop T. D. Jakes explains the concept of purpose in his bestselling book *Destiny: Step into Your Purpose.* In his book, Jakes explains that your purpose is directly influenced by your instincts, and that the two are predicated by your destiny in life. In a slightly differing perspective than Jakes', Rick Warren's commentary *What on Earth Am I Here For?* emphatically contends that Purpose is not about oneself, but it is rather directly connected to God and his plans for our lives. And lastly, in the book *Purpose Awakening: Discover the Epic Idea that Motivated Your Birth,* Touré Roberts's perspective on purpose represents a middle ground between the views of Jakes and Warren. Roberts concedes that while Purpose is grounded and begins with God, it is something that must be translated into real-world terms.

While it is surely not an obscure phenomenon, the concept of purpose and purposeful living spans across the ages of time and can be dated as far back to the times of the Bible. In fact, more modern-day perspectives on purpose is well aligned with the spiritual perspective in that both require an ability to deeply examine the inner meaning and significance of our lives and the importance of ourselves to others. It is something that God intended in the first place. More specifically, purpose is the primary motivational factor that influences and shapes our life's decisions, behaviors, and goals.

While some may argue with the contrary, the act of finding our life's purpose puts us on a deep path of self-discovery and forces us to see the reflection of ourselves staring back in the mirror. It requires a certain level of personal transparency, optimism, and faith in others, and the will power to sustain ourselves during times of challenge. By default, it helps us to define who we are and who we will become ultimately. It helps to answer the charge that is placed on our lives - *What we should be doing instead of what we are doing.* As indicated by T.D. Jakes, it helps to understand why and for what reason we were born, hence helping to define and shape our destiny.

Over the years, I've come to learn that purpose is not rooted and grounded in what we can see, but in what we feel—a sentiment shared by Touré Roberts. It is the thing that wakes us up each morning and keeps us pushing towards being better and doing better, not only for ourselves, but also for those we are accountable for and the ones who depend on us. I firmly believe that there is no coincidence in purpose, and everything that happens in life is pre-designed to be that way, whether the outcome is good or bad.

To truly understand the true meaning of purpose will require a shift in mindset. To be more specific, you must be willing and be able to change how you perceive yourself and the things and people around you. But, be aware that changing your mindset does not require you to change the person you are. You must remember that you were created for a purpose and a reason. Changing who you are to accommodate your relationship with Purpose is sure to make you fail at your discovery of purpose. The shift in mindset must occur in conjunction with making the necessary changes to your life to ensure that you are fulfilled.

So, what does it mean to make the necessary changes to your life? Making necessary changes to your life to realize your purpose requires you to remove roadblocks that will prevent you from achieving your goal. While Purpose itself is not a goal, finding it and forming a relationship with her is. The roadblocks could include one or more of the following things:

1. *An Identity Crisis* - The inability to see yourself for anything other than what you currently are. At such a

stage, you have somehow lost your luster and your love for yourself. You no longer feel worthy and consumed by your feelings of uncertainty.

2. *Lost Hope and Fear* - The inability to see past your own pain to look forward to the life "expectations" you have set for yourself or those that are subsequently pre-set for you. You lose your ambition, drive, and motivation. You no longer aspire or desire to do the things that make you happy. And, you fear rejection and disappointment.

3. *Impatient Growth* - The inability to wait for your breakthrough. You grow weary and become annoyed that everyone around you might be moving, and, yet, you remain stagnant.

4. *Thinking that Everyone who follows You is For You* - The inability to discern who is loyal and are contributors to your purpose. You think that everyone you encounter will share the same goals, perspectives, passions, and desires as you.

Bad All by Herself

Like twins, many people think that our good friends, Passion and Purpose, are one and the same, almost as if they are synonymous to each other. Some even tend to believe that they share the same qualities and symbolic meanings. Those same people will emphatically tell you that you cannot have one without the other. I used to be one of those believers, infatuated by my own desires, personal inhibitions, and selfish goals. However, that assumption could not have been much further from the truth—a truth that I would ultimately have to reconcile with if I was to finally denounce the fallacies I once believed. And, while Passion and Purpose may surely complement each other, much like their own unique characteristics and personal attributes, they differ in every way imaginable. They can only be reconciled by understanding who and what they truly are. In fact, Purpose does not need Passion to shine; she's bad all by herself.

It took me years to become one with my own Purpose. Like a baby who rejects her mother's breasts for the first time, or the mother who refuses to love the child she carried for the past nigh month, I rejected my Purpose at every turn. I was not overly excited about entertaining the thought of her presence in my life. It was not that I feared her or that I did not want her. However, just like so many of you, I did not spend enough time in getting to know her. I could not find my quiet place—that place where your mind is clear enough to see things or people for who and what they really are. Nor could I sit still long enough to hear her voice or feel her presence in my life. I was consumed by Passion, who kept me within her unrelenting grasps, moving from one adventure to the next. While I enjoyed the presence of Passion in my life, I had to let her go so that I could breathe, live, and allow Purpose to really have her turn in my life.

Unlike Passion, Purpose is an intentional representation of an obligation to self, almost as if you owed yourself a favor. Let me ask you this. When was the last time you gave yourself an IOU or wrote yourself a love letter? When was the last time you put yourself before others or said "no" to others so that you could say "yes" to yourself? Purpose is the validation of your existence, and it is the primary reason for every encounter that you will ever have. Some call it destiny, while others call it fate. But, despite its hidden objective, Purpose is the end of the beginning, and the beginning of the end to your life goals. It is a direct promise of what God has in store for you, and it is a part of the immaculate plan over your life. Consider it as a reward for the many sacrifices (notice that I did not say "compromises") you have made and the diligence it took for you to become one with self. Now, by no stretch of the imagination am I suggesting that in order for you to find your Purpose, it is necessary to become one with solely yourself. But, have you ever known anyone to apologize for finding and walking in their Purpose? Have you ever heard such a person say "Take this back! I don't want it"? This is what makes surrendering to Purpose so important.

Unfortunately, many people fail to surrender to Purpose, because they are not committed to her. In fact, they even refuse to date her. Moreover, they are unable to identify with her and are unwilling to accept her simply because she gets in the way of our everyday life, the everyday that we are yet to see. In fact, I would even argue that some even fear her. However, the irony in it all is that surrendering to Purpose should never warrant any special conditions or require you to do the extraordinary to find her and be with her. More importantly, it is not a prerequisite to finding your happiness and peace. If you think you have to go through pain to find your life's Purpose, you would be mistaken there as well.

Purpose is like a long-lost love, the kind of love that some will experience only once in a life time. It is that kind of love that you probably should not have had in the first place. It is that sticking kind of love. Holding on to things and people who serve you no purpose is like holding onto smoke. Soon, it too will dissipate and ultimately disappear completely from sight. When it comes to matters of the heart, Purpose is the driving force behind every beat. Everything else is superficial to the senses, which, by way of definition, some call lust. However, with Purpose, the swell inside your chest can be so severe that it snatches the air with every breath that you take.

The lesson here is that Purpose is not some arbitrary coincidence or some made-up romance. You don't just stumble upon her and make her yours accidentally. Truth be told, Purpose is a tough girl to catch, and she is not easily persuaded or influenced. You cannot buy her, nor can you simply smile in her face and expect her to give you back a glance of gratitude. You must remember that she's bad all by herself and does not need your help. She is the 'W' in your who and why as well as the 'H' in your how. She's the magic in the relationship that you have with her, and she will never apologize for always wanting more. In fact, she will only accept the best from you.

Purpose, Where Art Thou?

Many people miss out on the opportunity to find their purpose because they don't sit still long enough to realize it. When I was 22 years of age, I remember being in constant search for something so much greater than myself. But, as previously indicated, I could not put my finger on where the gaps were and what I had been missing. At that time, I used to think that I was positioned to accomplish everything I had planned. After all, I had a good job, met the love of my life, and was on my way to completing yet another degree.

I kept busy all the time, setting up my life for the next big thing. When Purpose did finally enter my life, it took me a while to realize that she was what I was missing. She had become a permanent fixture in my everyday life. I was no longer guided by Passion. Now, it was Purpose whom I'd let lead the occasions. All of the bumps and bruises I had encountered along the way had positioned me to really appreciate the value she had brought to our relationship. No longer was I a slave to the highs and lows that Passion would bring me, for what was brewing inside of me was more than I had ever thought I'd be able to enjoy. Not only did she make me a better person, but she began to define me, and people could see her. And now, they finally saw me as well, from miles away. She gave me courage to live in truth and speak my own truth unapologetically and without having any doubts.

However, finding Purpose can be tricky, and if you do not sit still long enough to listen for her, she might just pass you by. The psychology behind finding your purpose begins with a realization that you, alone, are not the sole beneficiary of your own purpose. It belongs to the others around you as well. Much of the literature on purpose suggests that you must have a relationship with God in order to find your purpose, for it is He who will reveal what your true calling is and how you should go about finding it. After you've reconnected with your spiritual self and have sought guidance and direction from God, you must consider the actions you must take to ensure that you are living, walking, and breathing in your purpose.

Now, the question that remains is that how do we get there? How do we get to the point where we are living our most purposeful life? The answers to these questions are simple. *Do what you love. Do what's most important to you. And, don't be afraid to stretch the boundaries of your imagination. Stay focused and firm on what you believe. But, be open to change and new perspectives.* Sounds easy enough, right? Wrong!

The problem with most adults is that they spend so much time deliberating on the consequences of their actions and what others might think of them that they forgo a rational train of thought to just simply do what needs to be done. Now, I am in no way suggesting that you make risky and rash decisions, but I am encouraging you to think about the time you spend in trying to digest how you are going to move towards your purpose. To elaborate further, we try to live the best possible life imaginable as children. For some of us, we had very few worries outside of our normal childhood inhibitions. Everything was new and exciting. We dared to dream and dreamed to dare. We did not concern ourselves much with the strategy for riding a bike, or how we were going to master our next steps. We just rode that bike until we stopped falling over. We rode until we mastered it, because we truly enjoyed the thoughts of what it would be like to ride alongside the other neighborhood kids.

While it can be tricky, finding your purpose does not have to be a difficult task. In fact, all it truly requires is an open mind, action, and resilience. Keep in mind that everything that you do or will ever do should be aligned with your life's purpose.

Your 5-Step Surrender Plan

So, are you prepared to surrender to Purpose? In doing so, you will be required to have a unique understanding of who and what she means to you. For some, Purpose is an action preceded by some life-altering event, or a situation they've found themselves in. While for others, it is closely aligned with some tragic event that led them to take an action or step out on a leap of faith. Despite what purpose means to you, you must prepare to surrender to it if you are seeking a fulfilled life, driven by meaning, happiness, and perspective.

As such, your surrender plan should include consideration of the following things:

1. ABANDON THE LIES YOU KEEP TELLING YOURSELF

Lying to oneself is the carefully crafted lie you've been telling yourself for years. People spend a lifetime convincing themselves of the things that never happened, or, for that matter, things that will never happen. They superficially construct a lie around what they want to happen, and, in some cases, they even believe that it has happened. The tragedy in creating those lies about yourself is that if you are not prepared for the consequences of keeping up with your lies, your lies will become all consuming, and you'll never be able to distinguish your reality from it. With every word you speak comes the consequences of those words, not just for you but for others as well.

You've rehearsed the same old story that you've been telling yourself for years. You know that story which is only true to the newest person you told it to. Lying to yourself about staying in a relationship you are aware that you should abandon. Lying to yourself about the man you should leave and all the reasons why you should stay. Lying to yourself about the problems you might have with your children. Lying to yourself about the successes you've had. Abandon those lies and begin walking in your truth.

2. REJECT THE PAST AND ACCEPT THE FUTURE

Ever found yourself fueled by the emotions of the past? Perhaps, it's an old fling that has you captivated in the thought of being with him or her again. It may even be the feeling of defeat or failure from losing a job that you loved. It could be a feeling of regret for not accomplishing a goal that you set for yourself in the last year. Or, perhaps it is about overcoming a pain that someone has caused you more than twenty years ago. Despite what you might have experienced, it's a reason why the past is the past, and why you should work hard to keep it there. You must remember that the past will never come back. And, while your subtle, or even vivid, memories might take you there, the past is merely designed to teach you valuable lessons that should never be taken into your future.

Carrying your past into your future could have dire consequences for everything and everyone you encounter in your future. Spending countless nights and days revisiting the pain that the past has brought to you does no good for your present, much less your future. Rejecting the past positions you to grow through new experiences and embark upon your purpose.

3. ALLOW YOURSELF TO "FALL", NOT "FAIL"

Falling is the proverb of failure. In order to fall, you must lose your balance and be prepared for the stumble you will face. The reactions of people to their falling never fail to amaze me. Some people laugh it off and get back up as if it never happened in the first place. Some people become irate, upset, and even embarrassed that they've fallen. But, the funny part about falling is that it makes you miss steps for your actions. It helps you understand that mistakes happen, and the aftermath of that mistake is simply the fall itself. The lesson here is that it's alright to fall because you have the ability to get back up and try those same steps all over again. Of course, it might hurt, and the bumps and bruises you'll surely be left with will be less than desirable. However, this time, you will know how to fall without breaking your bones or fracturing your ego.

Failure is a part of the process of self discovery. Failure is the start of your victory, and it is the happy beginning of your future. With every life lesson come bouts of failure. As in the act of falling, if you are unwilling and unable to allow your failures to teach you, you are closing the doors to bountiful possibilities. You cannot become strong without putting in the work to build your stamina and muscle. And, I can guarantee that the act of falling will most certainly give you the stamina that you need to keep on pushing and get back up.

4. UNDERSTAND THAT POTENTIAL HAS NOTHING TO DO WITH PURPOSE

Potential is a one-sided phenomenon, one that is conditional upon whether or not you possess a quality that can be developed into something else. A teacher might say that one of their students has the potential to be a lawyer because they possess the ability to critically analyze facts and have great communication and oratorical skills. Some tend to confuse the two, thinking that they must see the potential in themselves in order to have a purpose. This line of reasoning could not be further from the truth. People do not walk in potential. They walk in Purpose. Some people are naturally driven by the ambitions they may have for the things and the people around them. So, that same teacher, while fostering that student's ability to be a lawyer, should seek to help that student find their ambitions in and for law. This is where many people go astray from their true purpose. They follow their abilities and forgo their ambitions while seeking careers. Perhaps, it's the monetary gain that drives those decisions. Perhaps, it's the notoriety and fame that drives them to think that they've found their calling. Despite their rationale, unlike potential, purpose is already pre-developed; it not a probable or a likely phenomenon.

5. CREATE CONDITIONS FOR HER TO LIVE

One of the hardest things we, as humans, must do is forgo others for the sake of ourselves. Understanding that some of us are just simply built in a way to serve others before we serve ourselves, it's even more important that we find respite in the fact that life is an exchange. While there is nothing wrong in serving others, and I am surely not insinuating that you stop helping others, I need for you to understand that there are consequences for doing so.

So, I challenge you to think about the problems that could ensue by continually giving a part of yourself and not getting anything in return. How good are you to others if you are no good to yourself? How could you possibly bring happiness to others when you are not happy yourself? Many people sacrifice their own salvation, dreams, hopes, and even desires for the sake of others. This leads to a life of resentment, discomfort, and even depression.

In order for Purpose to thrive and grow, you must create and nurture the conditions for her to do so. You cannot surrender to your purpose if you are surrounded by people and things that don't pour and sow into you. You cannot surrender to your purpose if you are constantly playing defensive and offensive tackle in the game of life. And, you cannot surrender to your purpose if you are allowing others to take it away from you.

You must create an environment for your purpose to be realized. The process of doing so begins within you. Start by committing to be a happier person, debunking the myth that you must suffer in order to see the light. You must be prepared to clean your house of everything and everyone that directly or indirectly keeps you from dwelling in a place of peace and promise.

While they are not one and the same, surrendering to purpose should not be thought of as a sacrifice, or, for that matter, a compromise. It is an entitlement and a promise given to you by the Creator. It is already ordained and predestined to be a permanent fixture in your life. Your everyday walk should resemble God's plan for you. The trajectory of your life is dependent on your ability to become aware and familiar with your own purpose. I am hoping that you find solace in knowing that it is alright to not fully understand your purpose and that you use the surrender plan as a guide to get yourself there. As previously explained, it is true that there are going to be roadblocks that will delay your understanding. However, I challenge you to hold on, keep on pushing, and get ready for your breakthrough.

CHAPTER 7

Harnessing Power

"When I dare to be powerful - to use my strength in the service of my vision, then it becomes less and less important whether I am afraid."

—Audre Lorde

Do you remember the feeling that you had when you fell in love with your first superhero? Wonder Woman was my girl. It was played by the legendary Lynda Carter. Lynda Carter rose to fame in the 1970s as a beauty, hand sculpted from clay. She signified strength, passion, and courage for all starry-eyed little girls and boys. While the origins of Wonder Woman are just as intriguing as the story of how her super powers unfolded, Carter quickly became a beacon and a symbol of hope. However, underneath Carter's sweltering red, white, blue, and gold ensemble, she was just as angelic and accomplished as the character she played. She followed her passions, lived in her purpose, and eluded her power with every journey she made. She was a songwriter and a singer, a model and an actress. She was even, subsequently, crowned Miss World and was given the title of the Most Beautiful Woman in the World. She defied the rhetoric of traditional feminism and walked in her own truth—a truth that many women seek to embody today.

Having a friendship with Power can be equated to having superpowers that are possessed by some of our most cherished characters in childhood comic books and TV shows. In fact, all superheroes, both past and present, have some form of heightened awareness that they were either born with or given at some point in their lives. The Kryptonite was bestowed upon Superman, the Green Lantern was given a Power Ring, and the Black Panther ate of a heart-shaped herb to gain his powers. And, while Batman was not given any traditional superpowers, he was born of and possessed some innate attributes that made him great, worthy of a superhero status.

Despite my infatuation with superheroes, like many, I lacked the understanding of what true power was. I could only express how it made me feel and what I thought it could do. It took me years to harness and understand my relationship with Power. In fact, I did not experience her until I was well into my adult years. Even then, my experiences and relationship with her was a little fuzzy. She was forced upon me like a tidal wave hitting an open shore line. It dwelled inside of me like a burning bush. And, just like the characters in our most favored superhero novels, I did not realize the depths of what power could do.

In an effort to understand Power, it is essential to dive deep into some of the varying perspectives that are offered to explain how it came to be and what it signifies. It is one thing to relish in its impact on the situations and circumstances we find ourselves, and it is a different thing to harness the opportunities it truly affords us.

The first perspective can be gleaned from a theoretical and pervasive background. As children, some were taught that having Power was something bad, since it was historically associated with pain. It was believed that whoever had it controlled the masses and bestowed anguish amongst those within its grasps. Some began to understand it as an influence that one might have over others to get them to do what they so desire, or it was used, simultaneously, as a suppression tool. With varying degrees of complexity, many wars have been fought in the name of Power in order to gain control over the people, their possessions and land. The history of the enslavement of African descendants, and the oppression of their predecessors through racism and discriminatory laws as well as the Jewish Holocaust of World War II, and the religious oppression and intolerance in China highlight the magnitude of the contentions of Power in different nations all across the world. While there is surely some validity to this point of view, having a relationship with Power can be a beautiful thing as well.

Unlike the most common theoretical perspectives of Power, which rises from human intuition, ideology, and control, a second, and perhaps a more reasonable, explanation can be found from a Biblical standpoint. The Biblical approach to understanding Power is that is it nothing more than the strength and ability to accomplish something greater than oneself. In different versions of the Bible, Power is defined as something miraculous in nature, demonstrated by the many blessings that Jesus bestowed upon the sick, the dying, and the damned. It is further illustrated by the works of the Holy Spirit and its union with the Trinity.

A third perspective on Power can be examined in light of the scientific insinuation that describes Power in terms of time. More specifically, the scientific description contends that energy or the speed at which work is done or completed begets the manifestation of Power.

Despite how it is defined or the perspectives that are shared, Power is one of those necessary evils in this thing we call life. She is not to be confused with egotistical, self-centered behavior, but she must be understood as a consequence of your willingness to step out on faith and experience the greatness in you. It is often in our darkest moments that we dwell and call upon our relationship with Power to help us persevere. However, understanding your relationship with Power can be very tricky and downright risky at times. In order to harness your Power, you must be willing to do the unthinkable, and you must unapologetically make the decision to stand even when you have doubts about the consequences that might ensue. Power is only ignited when you are truly following Passion and have surrendered yourself to Purpose. She rounds out the dynamic trio.

Identifying Where Power Comes From

Our ability to harness Power is indicative of our capability to not only define what it truly means, but it requires us to intimately understand where it is coming from. Over the years, I've been called many things. One of them is "*Powerful*". I'm not sure at what point in my life or career I became worthy of such admiration, but I carry it with pride, and, more importantly, I use it responsibly. Doing so requires me to understand when it is the right time for me to tap into her and use her to my advantage. It's equally important for me to use her with good judgment and guidance from my friends, Passion and Purpose. However, in order for me to accomplish such a feat, I must clearly become one with where my Power is coming from at that time and in that moment. Just like the more traditional perspective on Power, if I fail at accomplishing a certain task, my efforts are often misguided, and it can be detrimental to those I love or to the people who support and endorse me.

Much like our superheroes of the past and present, our ability to harness true Power stems from a variety of things. It can be harnessed and evoked as a result of some special need, a situation we may find ourselves in, circumstances we are forced to face and go through, or by mere feelings and emotions. All of these things drive the extent to which we elude and call upon our Power to take control. While it is not required, I suggest that you take a quick moment to write down your answers to the following questions. If your answers to these questions have more than one occurrence, it is time to evaluate the instances and the reasons for which you are calling upon Power.

- How many times have you let your emotions consume you so much that you are unable to make sound and rational decisions?

- How many times have you allowed the mistakes of others to dictate the path or direction you ultimately take?

- How many times have you been in a heated argument and unleashed the wrath of God on someone?

- How many times have you been in a position to lead and refused to step up and exhibit your Power fearing that you would fail?

- How many times have you created a disaster in a relationship because you refused to act out your role?

As you assess your relationship with Power, don't be confused or scared by what she is trying to show you. Rather, you should be very afraid of what she will do for and to you. When I first stepped out on Power and trusted her to consume me, I embraced her like a friend. An understanding of where you are drawing your Power from will help you know how to channel her and ensure that you are positioned to accept accountability for the consequences, both positive or negative, that might ensue. It is your responsibility to absorb the impact of your power so that others around you will not be bitten by it or feel the impact of your misguided use of it.

Many people tend to think that in order to tap into their Power, or even have a relationship with her, they must be given the opportunity to show it or they must be placed in position for it to come out. Do you think Opra, Tyler Perry, Beyonce, or anyone else who has discovered this enigma truly cares about opportunities to exhibit their Power? If you answered yes, you would be incorrect. They, including myself, do not seek opportunities to display our Power; we create the opportunities for them to be displayed.

When I realized that Power was somewhat forgiving to my inability to appropriately handle her, I began shifting my mindset towards bridging any gaps that might have previously existed between Passion, Purpose, and Power. This is an essential step in identifying where Power comes from. However, where many people get it wrong is in thinking that Power is some hidden gem that needs to be sheltered or even protected. While she needs none of the aforementioned things, she must be controlled and held accountable. We will explore how to "Control Power" in the following section. The tragedy of such beliefs is that people never reach their full potential by ignoring the signs that she gives to them.

I learned it the hard way that not being able to channel my Power appropriately created a windfall of confusion and misinterpretation from those I loved. In recent years, I've come to understand that there are four stimuli in our lives that help us to identify with Power. Some may sound familiar, but they require a deeper understanding to truly know what they mean. While we may not recognize them at the very onset, we certainly feel them and call upon them when the necessity arises. Those four areas are given as follows:

1. Systemic Stimulation - Those things that are perpetuated by our internal or external environments, such as prisons or the judicial system.

2. Professional Stimulation - Those things, people, challenges, and opportunities in our careers or on our jobs that evoke changes in our work ethics, values, and morals.

3. Social Stimulation - Our social interactions and engagements with others around us.

4. Personal Stimulation - Our need for growth and development, success and relationships.

For those who need it, and to put it in perspective, the following section examines four concrete reasons to explain the triggers of your ability to harness your Power. More specifically, they will help you to understand *where* you are drawing your Power from.

Success and Failure

The most obvious way to find or draw upon Power is during times of success and failure. Since success and failure are oftentimes equated to and used simultaneously to describe a victory and defeat respectively, it's relatively simple to surmise that Power is an outcome of the two. However, this could not be further from the truth. It is only in some cases that Power is delivered and transferred during times of success and failure, victory and defeat. It is not a direct outcome of the two.

To illustrate this point, I would like to give an example. Think about all the countless wars that the US has fought and won or has been defeated. While there is conflicting evidence to suggest that the US has won countless wars or has perceived victories, the only true recorded victory of war was during Operation Desert Storm. However, even with that victory, the US did not become a Power authority in or to Kuwait. In fact, the US showed its superiority by solely helping to expel Iraqi forces from Kuwait. But, the US did not take indefinite control over the territory. Now, there are obviously some unique differences between taking Power to control a nation and taking Power to control an organization or even a group of people or a single person. But, the concept remains the same.

I've had the pleasure of meeting many successful and dynamic women in my entrepreneurial journey. Some of those women were game changers, ground-breakers, and what we call disruptors in their respective industry spaces. Some of them were working hard to pave the way for other women who desired success or merely needed a platform to shine. Although their varying differences were clear, they had one thing in common—they took their friend, Power, wherever they went, and she propelled them like a bullet leaving its chamber.

Naturally, you feel empowered when you are successful, and when you feel empowered, you subsequently feel powerful. At least, that is the mantra for some. But, this too could not be further away from the reality that most successful people experience. In fact, it is just the opposite.

Like many women in my position, as a successful woman business owner, I struggled with the differences between being successful and being powerful. More specifically, I struggled to understand as to when it was appropriate to allow my Power to overshadow my success. While I enjoyed being successful, I was afraid to show just how powerful I was. I was afraid of failure and did not recognize what I was doing to my visions and dreams. I worked tirelessly to build relationships that were mutually beneficial, and I was stigmatized for merely being a woman. I didn't want to turn people off by seemingly coming across as too forceful, and rarely did I want to say no. I was a people pleaser, and I would do anything to ensure that those around me knew my potential and respected my position.

So, I downplayed my relationship with Power and allowed myself to fall victim to what others thought I should be. Subsequently, I was pushed and pulled in all the wrong directions. I made unwise decisions—decisions that were in the best interest of others and not me. I took risks that I would have never otherwise thought to make, and I did things that I really did not want to do. I played second fiddle to those who were less accomplished than me, and I let go of money-making opportunities for the fear that I'd never get them.

My earlier successes came at a great cost, because I did not bother to take my friend, Power, along for the ride. I hid her behind closed doors, afraid at what she might do if she ever came out. However, being determined to not repeat the same cycle as my success began to grow, I grew stronger in my friendship with Power. No longer was I afraid to let her shine, take over, and make decisions in the best interests for the both of us.

What I soon realized was that it was not the success or failure that I was most afraid of, it was Power. As women, it is direly importantly that you not only position yourself for success and greatness, but that you use your relationship with Power to get what you want, when you want it, and how you want it. To put it simply, don't allow your inhibitions with Power to distort the truths that are right in front of you. Success does not make you powerful. It only serves to makes you more diligent, relentless, and sharp. However, it must be accompanied by your friend, Power. She is the one that will make you fight for your success and see you through to your greatness. She is the one who will pave the way and keep you balanced and positioned.

Oftentimes, we spend so much time in trying to shift through the good, negate the bad, and beautify the ugly that we forget what is most important.

Trauma and Pain

Like many women, I was confused by my experiences with Power. But, I soon realized that there was one area in my life where Power always seemed to show up. It was during those hard times, especially when I was experiencing some type of trauma and pain in my relationships with others.

I remember it like it was yesterday. I was just 7 years old. He'd pick me up out of my bed, lay me beside him, and as the elders would say, "He'd have his way". I vividly remember the rage and pain on my mother's face and the many tears she cried.

I remember him rendering his guilt before the courts, specifically saying, "If the girls say I did it, I did it". I remember the look on his face, as they took him away. And, I remember the silence in the court room as we left to establish a new normalcy.

But, this story of pain did not end there. His family disowned us and cursed our family for the secret we revealed. They defended their brother and said that we were lying. Without hesitation or remorse, they treated us like we were step children, mere half breeds to their throne. And, to this day, I am yet to speak a word to anyone he calls family, except by way of accidentally meeting a cousin at my maternal mother's family function. But, this was not for the lack of trying.

To help bring closure to my experience, when I turned twenty-five years old, I went on a search to find my paternal family. I managed to find and obtain the telephone numbers of two sisters and a brother. One sister was very receptive to the idea of a potential meeting. We even scheduled a dinner. But, the other sister was not so willing to entertain the slightest thought of an encounter. The unwilling sister convinced the other not to allow a reunion, and I was subsequently cursed out and blackballed once again from his family. My last and final attempt to bring solace to my experience was when I found and located his mother—my grandmother. She was more than willing to finally have an opportunity to meet. But, once again, the unwilling sister intervened and stopped the reunion. She specifically said, "Leave my mother alone". I've even heard "the only reason you have come back is to get my brothers money". The heartbreak was unimaginable, and the old wounds unexpectedly opened up once again. Now, here is one of those instances where I could have unleashed the wrath of God on someone.

It wasn't until I was much older that I felt compelled to share in writing this story of sexual abuse by the man I had once loved so dearly. He stripped me of my innocence, and his actions tore me away from his family. Granted that it was a family I vaguely knew, however, he had taken my young and growing Power—a Power I didn't know existed. While I did not know it back then, this experience became the set up for the woman I've become today.

Here is where the story comes to a full circle. Despite all his lies, deception, and deceit, I worked through all of that pain, found my strength, and took my power back. I moved on with my life—a chance that many young ladies who share the same experience never get a chance to do. If they had only taken the time to meet, they would have known that all I simply wanted was to let them know that "I forgive them".

"Forgiveness does not exonerate the perpetrator. Forgiveness liberates the victim. It's a gift you give yourself." – Bishop T.D. Jakes

As life went on, there was some pain indeed, even bits of resentment. But, in order for me to heal, I had to forgive the man who hurt me and thank God for the people who chose to chase me away. It is because of them that my mother got the sole opportunity to groom and shape a superstar. For all the women reading this story, I want to encourage you to FIGHT through your pain, FORGIVE your oppressors and those who have done you wrong, and REWARD them by becoming the best you that you can be.

So, today, I want to say "Momma, we did it!". I know I've made and continue to make you proud. And, all I want to say to his family is that I don't need your mother's love or your money. I've made my own millions! The moral of the story is to stop blaming others for the pain they have caused you. Acknowledge it, forgive it, and let it go.

Fear and Courage

There is no room for fear when you are working towards harnessing your Power. However, feelings of fear are the conduit in which Power has an opportunity to rear her pretty or ugly head. Being doubtful brings about feelings of anxiety, and anxiety, in turn, stirs fear. When this combination is well aligned, Power can do one of two things for you. You will lose her all together, succumbing to your fears and lose the war, or you will use your fears to become empowered and exhibit your courage.

When I find myself in a state of fear, I've learned to tap into my innermost Power to help me absorb the impact of those fears. While I consider myself to be a warrior, I must say that I find myself afraid at times to do many of things that I really want to do.

For my daughter's eleventh birthday, I took her to Hawaii, one of the most beautiful places on earth. While we were there, we partook in many of the local activities, including swimming in the ocean with unknown breeds of fish, and also what I assumed were sharks. However, it wasn't until my daughter decided to go parasailing that things really began to take wrong turn. While I enjoy a good thrill, the excitement of flying outside of an airplane while over water was more than what my nerves could handle.

As we sailed out to our parasailing location, I could see the fear in the eyes of my baby girl. She started shaking uncontrollably, and her teeth started to chatter. Realizing what we were about to do, she sat perfectly still gazing at the oncoming sunset that overlooked the Waikiki Bay. She had no idea that I was just as afraid. I was sweating from head to toe, and I had thoughts about just staying put on that boat, not even letting them strap me in. As we got further and further away from the shore, my heart began to pound, and my mind started playing tricks on me. I swore that I saw baby sharks in the water, swimming around the boat. But, as I looked into my baby's eyes, I knew in that very moment that I had to stay strong, find the courage to complete our adventure, and make her proud. So, I turned to her and said, "Baby girl, if you don't want to go up, we can sit right here on this boat." She looked at me, chattering through her teeth, and said, "Yes, mommy! I want to go." I saw my life flash before my eyes. But, I also saw the disappointment in my baby girl's face as we both sat in the boat, fearing to go up in the sky, dangling more than 100 ft off a sailing boat.

The boat assistant harnessed us up. We lay sideways off the moving boat, and in a matter of five seconds, we were mid-air. And, soon, we were in full flight. I closed my eyes tightly, took the hand of my baby girl, and said, "Look Nyla! We did it!" That day, my courage had a profound impact on me and my relationship with my daughter. It was at that moment that I became her Wonder Woman.

You see, oftentimes, we spend so much time in trying to fight fear that we neglect the very weapon we possess to destroy it. Fear is nothing more than an illusion that our mind portrays. It only becomes real when we allow it to take control of us. Now, don't get me wrong; I realize that some people may have some legitimate fears—fear of water, fear of snakes, fear of heights, and even fear of dying. But, when you have the courage to face those fears, your Powers ignite and help you to overcome your inhibitions or plight. Power, in this sense, gives you the courage to stand up to those fears, confront them face to face, and legitimize your position and stance in the situation.

Leadership and Obligation

I had been raised by a single mother in one of the toughest cities in New Jersey. When I was a child, my mother was clearly the figure of authority in our home. She undoubtedly held all the Power. After all, she was the primary breadwinner. She was the one who controlled all the money, and she was the one who set all the rules. She was not only the provider, but she was the caretaker as well. And, her primary responsibility was to ensure that we had all the things that we needed and some of the things that we wanted. She dictated our every move—where we went, who we hung out with, and, more importantly, how we would be raised. She played her position very well, and we dared not go against her word, for if we did that, we knew firsthand the Power she would unleash.

She was brave and grounded, protective and strong. She called on her friend, Power, every single day to get her through those darkest and bleakest moments in life. She worked two jobs, put my sister and me through private school, and always made the necessary sacrifices to make sure that we were positioned for greatness. Her relationship with Power was nothing short of amazing and beautiful. They shared a special bond. I could not understand or even begin to fathom how she was able to stay so focused through everything that she endured alone. She was a praying woman, and her sense of obligation to her children pushed her to do whatever she could to make our lives meaningful.

For my mother, it was her sense of obligation and her responsibility to her children that made her fall in love with Power. For the next thirty years, until her retirement, the two of them became inseparable. She never left home without her. While this story has a happy ending, there are countless others who were not so fortunate. For some, the ideology of having an authority figure at home had a totally different ending. Sometimes, feelings of obligation, combined with authority, can bring about negative consequences for those in the home. A prime example is an abusive father or mother. The weight of obligation becomes so unbearable that they use their relationship with Power to inflict pain and harm. Today, we call this mental and physical abuse.

But, understanding how feelings of obligation commands Power is only one part of the equation. It gets a little more complicated when Power is called upon in leadership. Positions and roles of leadership automatically give way for people to assume that they have an infinite and intimate relationship with Power, as if their friendship is owed to them. In fact, in some cases, they tend to believe that since they are in control, it is their duty to control everything and everyone around them. Have you ever had a job where your manager pulled the Power card on you?

Have you ever had a job where your manager would not let you be innovative and creative for fear that you'd outshine them? Have you ever had a manager who micromanages everything that you do because they do not trust your assumed outcome? In research, we call this an authoritative leadership style, whereby the leader strips his subordinates of all autonomy and directs and leads all their activities. The irony in this assumption is that even they have others around them thinking the very same thing.

I've only had a handful of jobs in my lifetime, two of which subsequently turned into careers. During my tenure as an employee to someone else, I learned three valuable lessons about Power. First, and perhaps the most important, is that I do not make a very good employee. Second, I'm not a big fan of the old paradigmatic models of leadership, which places more emphasis on Power and legitimating control. And third, I was better suited to play in the Power house than be a subordinate. This in no way depicts that I am more worthy to hold such a position. But, I can say that I have grown enough in my relationship with Power and know intimately what I can accomplish with her.

Good leaders understand the importance of introducing Power to their teams. They shy away from hiding her, and they would much rather share her with others. Much like Robert K. Greenleaf's theory of servant leadership (an evolving leadership paradigm), I propose that Power should be used to develop the people who face it, helping them flourish and grow. In thinking about our assessment of the superheroes earlier in this chapter, we have observed that the sole purpose of the Power that superheroes possess it either to enhance their abilities to do good or to do bad. Despite everything, what you must remember is that there is always a Power over the Power, and that Power is you.

Power Check: When to Summon Her

Now that we have an understanding of where Power comes from and under what circumstances she may surface, it is time to learn how to keep her in check and when you will need her. While we surely want her to shine, it is crucial that we hold her accountable, that she is responsible, and that she is ready when called upon.

Perhaps, one of the hardest things for people to do is keep our dear ole Power in check. Due to her tendency to overstep the boundaries in your life, it is critical that you keep her in check so that she does not wreak havoc on you and deter you from doing the things that you want to accomplish. There is a time and a place for everything, and your use of the gifts and advantages that Power brings is no different.

Ever since I was a little girl, I had the gift of the gab. I could talk the shoes off a horse and run circles around the most talented of them. I was filled with so much passion that I thought that I was completely invincible, and nothing could stop my hustle. I dared to dream, and my dreams were a dare. Beyond advice, I was the girl who everyone ran to when they needed that extra spark or that extra push. I was the one who would step out in front of a moving truck without having in any escape plan. I was just what I thought I wanted to be.

As my life began to come to a full circle and things became clearer for my life's purpose, I had to make some decisions about how I wanted to be perceived. Did I really want to be known as some power player, a boss chic? Did I really want to be held responsible and accountable for the success of others? The answers to these questions was a resounding "Yes". But, I had to figure out how I could maximize on the outcomes of this great feat. The most logical strategy was to reposition my relationship with Power and allow her to do what she did best. I needed her to be the voice for the voiceless and the strength for the powerless. I needed her to be courageous for the fearful and a role model for the aspiring and seeking. I needed her to become a reborn version of Wonder Woman.

Understanding when to summon your friend, Power, is just as important as understanding who she is and what she can do for you. As I sought to seek her assistance in accomplishing many of my life's goals, you too must know when to summon her to help you deliver on your greatness. While it is not all encompassing, there are several conditions and scenarios for which you will need to summon your friend, Power. She should be summoned when you find yourself at your weakest moments, or when you feel like you cannot go on. Those are the times when you need to work the hardest to bear down and push through those circumstances and fight the temptation to give up.

She should also be summoned when you find yourself in the middle of pursuing a dream. There will be many people along the way who will seek to keep you from reaching your goals. They will take your esteem and make you feel less than them. They will make you feel inadequate and unworthy. Don't be afraid to take Power to boardrooms and meetings. Take her with you when you are negotiating your financial stake in a business endeavor or for those who are working in other people's businesses, take her with you when it's time for that raise. Tap into her to show your quality, skill, knowledge, and expertise. Use her as the conduit to expel your greatness to others.

Your friendship with Power can also help you in broken relationships. Summon Power when you need the strength to leave. Allow her to be your voice and allow her to stand strong for you in the time of weakness. Many women stay in dangerous, abusive, and destructive relationships, not because they want to, but because they have not found the strength to fight back. Out of fear and by thinking that they are not strong enough, they succumb to their fears, allowing their circumstances to become all consuming. There goes that word again—fear! It is not good enough to simply say that it's going to get better, or that now is not the right time. It is always the right time to make a power move and power play. Stop bleeding through your pain and work on being the survivor in your own story. You've got to change your mindset, stand your ground, take responsibility and accountability for your own happiness, and break free of the him or her who is seeking to destroy you.

Lastly, seek the help of Power when you find yourself in a position to impact a positive change. If you think about the many great social change advocates and freedom fighters of our past and our present, you will see that there is one thing that they all shared in common. They shared a strong conviction to ensure that the injustice that others face are resolved. Great people like Martin Luther King Jr., Mahatma Gandhi, Rosa Parks, Marcus Garvey, Sojourner Truth, Nelson Mandela, and Angela Davis called on their friend, Power, to speak truth, bring light, and evoke progressive change for the many people they admired and loved. They called on their Power to help them overcome the hatred and senseless acts of prejudice and injustice to move forward in their purpose. Can you imagine a world where there would be no one to speak up for the change that we so desperately need in our communities, for our children and our future?

Don't Make It Complicated

As we've explored earlier, there are several nuances in understanding both your friendship and your subsequent relationship with Power. But, if you still don't know where to start from, I would offer only two golden rules for harnessing and tapping into your Power.

The first would be to clearly know where to find her. Since your power can come from different places, you must know where she shows up most often so that you are able to benefit from her presence. Ask yourself the following questions:

1. Does she show up when you are in pain or going through some type of trauma?

2. Does she show up when you feel fearful or need an extra bit of courage?

3. Does she show up when you are experiencing success or when you feel like you are about to fail?

4. Does she show up only when you are placed in a leadership role or during the moments when your obligations become all too consuming?

The second, and perhaps the hardest, is to know how to use her. Using Power to your advantage is the cornerstone of your relationship with her. Knowing how to use her and spend time with her will ensure that she provides the guidance that you need to overcome the challenges in reaching success with any endeavor that you embark upon or situations you find yourself in.

I want to encourage you to always prepare for war and be ready when the time comes for battle. You must understand that you may get disappointed along the way or even lose your fight, however, do not dwell on what you cannot control. Pick yourself up, dust yourself off, and allow your Power to take over in order to help you overcome. There is a fine line between control and Power, and if you allow her, she will surely gut you like a fish out of fresh water.

However, in the contrary, Power can be a beautiful thing. And, now that you've read this chapter, hopefully you now understand that it takes practice, discipline, and courage to see her show up and act out. I am hoping that you also learned that if you use her precariously, she will wreak havoc in everything that you do.

I've never been the type of person to pass out on a good challenge or a good fight. In fact, I marvel at the opportunities to do so, and I want to encourage you to do the same. Like our dear ole Marvel and DC comic superhero friends, we must embrace our Powers despite how and when they come.

I charge you to reflect on the superhero that you want to become or consider creating your own. Think about the special Powers that they might possess and determine which ones you might have. Clearly, we know that the powers given to our favorite superheroes are make believe. But, Powers of all kinds are transformational and transactional. They are a true representation of give and take. Whichever you choose, find ways to harness your Power by first learning where she might be lurking, and under what circumstances she might manifest herself. Second, be clever about how you keep her in check, and be careful not to water her down or shut her out. And lastly, study, practice, and master the two golden rules for harnessing Power. Not only will you be better equipped to recognize her, but you will also know how to appropriately handle and use her to your benefit and advantage.

CHAPTER 8

Final Notes for Following Passion, Surrendering to Purpose & Harnessing Power

Final Notes for Following Passion

Now that you have the directions for following your passion, I want to provide you with a bonus. In a video I posted, not too long ago on Instagram, I charged women to stop babysitting other people's feelings when they are moving toward their greatness. When you are working toward self-improvement and efficacy, it is imperative that you not allow outside influences to break your momentum, deterring you from the charge ahead of you. This includes the distractions and limitations you might even cause yourself.

The same principles apply when following your friend Passion. By now, you might have figured out that your friend Passion requires a lot of attention, focus, and care. You must be willing to stroke your relationship with her, if not for anything, but to establish a give and take. So, here are your notes for following Passion.

1) Having a relationship with Passion should not be painful. In fact, it could be a beautiful thing - a harmonious balance between your dreams and reality. So, stop putting limitations on yourself and stretch the realm of your feelings, emotions, needs, and desires.

2) Don't be afraid to show up and show out for your friend Passion. While she can be a little erratic at times, she will keep you full and thirsty, hungry for more of what she has to offer.

3) Your relationship with Passion is uniquely yours. No one will understand it or appreciate it more than you. In fact, those surrounded by you have no stake in the game and will confuse your relationship with Passion as some hobby or dream.

4) As previously indicated, don't let your relationship with Passion die. Don't put her on "don't disturb." She deserves a phone call from you every day.

5) Your relationship with Passion will evolve as you begin to understand your self-worth truly. I urge you to fall in love with yourself all over again to find it.

6) You must fight FOR your relationship with Passion. Notice I did not say "fight WITH" your friend Passion. While the two of you are very close, there will be times when your friendship will be tested. Competing priorities will try to keep you from her. But you must find time to spend with her. Every day you spend with her will be a gift and provide you with a new outlook on life and living.

A letter to my Friend Passion

Dear Passion,

Thank you for teaching me how to live and how to fall in love with myself all over again. Thank you for showing me that life can be full- filled with so much pleasure and joy. Thank you for the many roads we've traveled together and the life experiences we've shared. Thank you for dreaming for me, when no one else seemed to care. Thank you for our many sleepless and restless nights, as we lay awake envision our next big break. I am honored to call you sister and sometimes a foe because our life together is remarkably beautiful. So keep on dreaming for me Passion; don't ever let me go, I'm looking forward to seeing how much more we can grow.

Final Notes for Surrendering to Purpose

For many people, the thought of surrendering to something or someone can be daunting, scary and confusing. And, for others, it is a welcomed change. But your ability to fully surrender to your friend Purpose is an essential step toward reaching fulfillment and peace. Surrendering to Purpose implies that you are letting go of anything or anyone that is hindering your ability to follow God's plan for you. If you recall my earlier story at the beginning of this book, it wasn't until I completely surrendered to God and allowed Him to become the designated driver in my life, that things began to change. Not only was my mind clear but now I could the destiny that laid ahead.

Today, my life is so much more rewarding and fulfilling because I've reconnected with my friend Purpose. While it took some time for us to get on the same page, we are closer than we've ever been. She has shown me that there is no greater gift in life than to be able to pursue a complete ME.

But, despite all her greatness, I must share that she is not very forthcoming. You must be patient with Purpose. Sometimes she can take what will seem like forever to show you what she can do. You must allow her to pour and sew into you, without hesitation or regret. You must find the courage to trust her guidance and direction in your life. Many women fail at their relationship with Purpose because they refuse to accept that she is an instrumental figure in their lives. When you surrender to Purpose, you are emphatically doing what God has intended. Sometimes, we can get so caught up in our everyday lives that we neglect the one person in our lives that mean the most - YOU!

And finally, you did not meet Purpose by accident. In fact, there are very few instances in life where things happen by accident. Everything is perfectly designed just the way it was intended, even if you did not intend it to be that way. So remember that it was your friend Passion that introduced you to Purpose. And, sometimes you must bring the two together to have those tough conversations about what might be missing. However, in those conversations, it is essential that you bear your soul to her. Don't put up a facade or mask your true self from her. She is perhaps one of the few people you should let into your life.

A Letter to my Friend Purpose

Dear Purpose,

Purpose, thank you for teaching me humility and patience; without you, my life would have had very little meaning. Thank you for wrestling with me and helping me find my place of peace. I am forever indebted to your unyielding love for me and the way you always put things back into perspective. Thank you for reminding me that you are forever present and will still have a special place for me.

Final Notes for Harnessing Power

Over the years, my relationship with Power has come full circle. I had to learn to trust her and not be afraid to use her as a crutch when I needed that extra push to fight through pain, anxiety or fear. In fact, admittedly, I call her up when I'm about to close a business deal. I call her up when I'm trying to get out of a troubling situation I may have put myself in. And, I call her up when I am about to stand in front of a room to deliver a keynote speech. Yes, I still get major butterflies in front of large crowds.

Your relationship with Power will propel you to reach heights you've never reached before. Don't be afraid to identify with her and use her to defend off the negative feelings you might be experiencing. Let her be one of your solutions to fighting through brokenness. She will help you win the war against the things and people that are silently seeking to destroy you.

In this book, I gave you four areas - during times of success and failure, during times of trauma and pain, during times of fear and during times when your sense of obligation or leadership becomes all too consuming - in your life where she is sure to show up. The beauty of your relationship with Power is that you don't have to do much to find her. She is only a quick phone call away.

- Call on her if you are going through a terrible divorce.
- Call on her if you are being emotionally and physically abused.
- Call on her when you have landed an opportunity for a new job.
- Call on her when you need to let go of an addiction.
- Call on her when you've fallen into a state of depression.
- Call on her when your children are acting up.
- Call on her when you have to defend yourself again those who don't share the same sentiments as you.

The point is, don't close the door to her entry by being too humble. Allow her to do her job and be the friend that you need her to be. Trust me; she is much stronger than you think.

A Letter to my Friend Power

Dear Power,

I admire your strength, your drive and your ambition. Thank you for giving me courage, and for teaching me resilience and what it means to have conviction. Thank you for standing up for me when my legs refused to move and when my mouth failed to open. Thank you for allowing me to lean on you when I felt weak and thank you for taking care of things when they looked bleak. You are a fearless representation of God's plans for me.

Acknowledgements

Sisterhood, like most friendships, are not created equal. There are not many women who get to experience the joys of true sisterhood. So I'd like to acknowledge the contributions of four very special women in my life. They make up the passion that drives my ambitions, the purpose that guides my decision making and the power that forces me to forge forward in my quest for greatness. Veronica, my high school classmate, for more than 30 years our friendship has never been broken. Although we do not speak every day, I feel your presence in my life daily and thank you for your genuine love and unyielding support. Toni, Kamilah and Simone, thank you for always riding with and for me, inspiring and pushing me towards my passions. My relationships with you have helped to shape the woman I am and have taught me so much about the meaning of unconditional love. All of our lives are forever changed and more meaningful because we have each other. Each of you mean the world to me and in all of your authentic glory, you bring me so much joy.

My twin sister Talbatha, words cannot even begin to describe nor express the unique role you play in my life. While our destinies are far from the same, from birth your presence in my life confirms that I was created for a special reason, even if that reason was to simply be your sister. Thank you for your encouragement and more importantly, thank you for your unbiased support and love.

My mother Elaine, thank you for not clipping my wings and allowing me to soar and reach. Thank you for giving me the tools to be successful and teaching me that my purpose is just for me. I am forever indebted to your many sacrifices.

More importantly, Lord I thank you for allowing me the opportunity to follow my passions, find my purpose and walk in my power. Without you, my journey would be meaningless and incomplete.